The Counselor and the Law

Fourth Edition

By

Barbara S. Anderson

AMERICAN
COUNSELING
ASSOCIATION

THE COUNSELOR AND THE LAW
Fourth Edition

10 9 8 7 6 5 4

American Counseling Association
5999 Stevenson Avenue
Alexandria, VA 22304

Acquisitions and Development Editor
Carolyn Baker

Managing Editor
Michael Comlish

Cover design by Brian Gallagher

Library of Congress Cataloging-in-Publication Data

Anderson, Barbara S., 1952–
    The counselor and the law / by Barbara S. Anderson. — 4th ed.
      p. cm.
    Rev. ed. of: The counselor and the law / by Bruce R. Hopkins, Barbara S. Anderson. 3rd ed. ©1990.
    Includes bibliographical references.
    ISBN 1-55620-152-4
    1. Student counselors—Legal status, laws, etc.—United States. 2. Counseling—Law and legislation—United States. 3. Counselors—Legal status, laws, etc.—United States. I. Hopkins, Bruce R. The counselor and the law. II. Title.
KF4192.5.G8H67   1996
344.73'017613712022—dc20
[347.30417613712022]
                                           96-11766
                                           CIP

CONTENTS

PREFACE

More than 15 years ago the American Personnel and Guidance Association (APGA) first published a small book entitled *The Counselor and the Law* to help counselors, mostly school counselors, understand the potential areas of liability they might encounter in their professional practices. Since that time the counseling profession has undergone a significant transformation and has achieved recognition of its new status through state licensing and certification. Two changes to the name of the association during this period, from APGA to the American Association for Counseling and Development (AACD), and to the current American Counseling Association (ACA), reflect this dynamic progression. These changes similarly highlight a critical aspect of our law: It is a dynamic, ever-evolving process that reflects transformations in our society at large, not a stagnant, staid structure that remains the same over time. Of course, the essential framework remains intact, but as new situations arise, the law rises to meet new demands and new ideas.

For the counselor, as for lawyers, it is impossible to know all there is to know about the law or to predict the outcome of any case brought to court. Changes in technology are presenting new challenges in record keeping and confidentiality. How does the duty to warn comport with the need to maintain client confidences? What is the impact of managed care on professional practice? Are counselors affected by the Americans With Disabilities Act? What about reporting unprofessional conduct when the information comes from your client? When should a counselor refer a client to another professional? These are only a few of the issues that now arise in practice. ACA has adopted a new *Code of Ethics and Standards of Practice* to guide counselors in conducting and managing their daily practice. This fourth edition covers these topics, as well as a host of other changes in the laws affecting counselors that have occurred in the 5 years since the last edition.

Further complicating the issue, the law as it applies to counselors varies from state to state and from situation to situation. State certification and licensing requirements impose different obligations on professionals. Court decisions also vary widely depending on the particular judges involved in the case, how well the case is presented, and the particular facts of each case. Through all this professional counselors, as other professionals, have an obligation to keep themselves up-to-date on relevant issues.

In this book an attempt is made, as in the previous editions, to provide a general guide for counselors to conduct their practice in a legal and ethical manner by outlining the broad legal pitfalls that could trap unwary or uninformed professional counselors. General principles of law are set out together with the ACA's *Code of Ethics* to give professional counselors an overview of the laws and ethical considerations that affect them. The book is not intended to be an in-depth treatment of legal or ethical standards, but it should enable counselors to spot important issues as they arise in practice. *The Counselor and the Law,* Fourth Edition, is meant to be a resource, together with the *ACA Code of Ethics and Standards of Practice* (1995) (see Appendix A), the *ACA Ethical Standards Casebook,* Fifth Edition (1996), the ACA Legal Series, and other publications yet to come, to guide counselors in making decisions that have an impact on their professional practice. Many of the hypothetical cases presented are drawn from case law and practice, as well as the *ACA Ethical Standards Casebook*. The principles enunciated in these examples apply to all facets of the counseling profession and should be examined carefully to see how they relate to particular specialties or situations. As with previous editions of this book, the purpose is not to tell counselors how to counsel their clients, but to establish, as clearly as possible, the permissible bounds of conduct within which the counselor can perform his or her job effectively and legally.

Similarly, this book is not intended as a substitute for the considered opinion and advice of a personal lawyer or the lawyer of an employer, who may also be available for advice concerning the particular circumstances of a case in the context of local laws and customs. Counselors who are covered by professional liability insurance through the ACA Insurance Trust, Inc., also may seek risk management guidance from an attorney through the Trust's Risk Management Hotline. It must be emphasized again that each counselor has the obligation to become familiar with state and local laws and customs of the profession, as well as the *ACA Code of Ethics*, and to give reasoned, informed consideration to the situations that may present themselves in day-to-day practice.

ACKNOWLEDGMENTS

I am grateful to the American Counseling Association and to many members of the staff of ACA for their continued dedication to professional counselors and their clients. It is ACA's emphasis on protecting clients, while firmly establishing the identity and competence of professional counselors, that has established counseling as a profession recognized by certification and licensure.

As I gathered material for this fourth edition I was greatly assisted by Carolyn Baker, acquisitions and development editor, Paul Nelson, executive director of the ACA Insurance Trust, Inc., and Sylvia Nisenoff, ACA librarian. My sincere thanks to each of them. Bert Bertram and Nancy Wheeler's seminars on the "Legal Aspects of Counseling" were very helpful in targeting new areas to add to this edition, and I also appreciate their willingness to review the text. I am grateful for their comments and support.

Most of all, I sincerely appreciate the support of my family, Alan, Chris, and Brian, who have taught me much about love, commitment, and patience.

ABOUT THE AUTHOR

Barbara S. Anderson is a lawyer admitted to practice in Virginia and the District of Columbia. She is a graduate of the George Washington University (BA, 1973) and received her law degree in 1982 from the Washington College of Law of the American University. She co-authored the previous editions of *The Counselor and the Law* and writes extensively for a variety of publications, including the *Section 504 Compliance Handbook* and the *ADA Compliance Guide*. Barbara Anderson was formerly assistant director of the National Association of Student Financial Aid Administrators, and she continues to work on education- and disability-related issues in the community and in her legal practice.

CHAPTER 1

THE COUNSELING PROFESSION

An estimated 250,000 to 300,000 professional counselors work in America in a variety of health care, education, and social service settings. Although no specific body of law governs the profession exclusively, courts and state legislatures have made inroads in this area in recent years. In the mid-1970s the first edition of this book focused primarily on the potential legal concerns of counselors working in schools. There were few court decisions directly involving school counselors and even fewer state or federal statutes to provide guidance about the limits of permissible conduct toward student counselees. Counselors were viewed by the public—and viewed themselves—as belonging to an emerging profession. Lacking clear legal direction or a code of professional ethics until 1961, many well-meaning counselors ventured into counseling situations that had serious legal ramifications.

At that time, for example, limited school budgets did not support the growing demand for professionals such as school psychologists and social workers, so school counselors were called upon frequently to fulfill these roles. Because school counselor job descriptions did not include providing therapeutic services, as is the case for psychologists and psychiatrists, the demand for increased services from counselors created a number of potential legal pitfalls. Civil rights and confidentiality problems further complicated the issue. The heavy emphasis of helping counselees from a humanistic viewpoint, which necessitates a very personal relationship, was also examined as a potential basis for legal liability in cases where a student might be harmed. Finally, school counselors had conflicting responsibilities to students, their parents, and society as a whole, of which the school is an important part. These issues were addressed in the first edition of *The Counselor and the Law* to give some direction to guidance and other school counselors.

The counseling profession of the 1990s is significantly different from the "emerging profession" of the 1960s and early 1970s. Perhaps the most striking differences lie in the variety of employment settings where counselors practice and in the types of human concerns with which they now deal. Although many practicing counselors are still employed by educational institutions, both public and private, growing numbers of counselors also work in mental health agencies, community agencies, correctional facilities, public employment agencies, rehabilitation agencies, health care facilities, private practice, business, and industry. They help clients with concerns such as personal and social development; career and educational guidance; mental health; hygiene; physical and vocational rehabilitation; unemployment or underemployment; reentry into school or the work force; substance abuse; marriage and family planning; parenting; aging; child, spouse, or elder abuse; and spirituality. In short, virtually all facets of personal, social, career, and educational needs are addressed by the various professionals who practice under the title "counselor." Most professional counselors have master's degrees in counseling and may also be licensed or certified by the state in which they work or by a national board, such as the National Board for Certified Counselors.[1]

Counseling now enjoys other hallmarks of a mature profession as well. In 1983 the American Personnel and Guidance Association responded most visibly to the growth and change in the profession by changing its name to the American Association for Counseling and Development (AACD) and subsequently to the American Counseling Association (ACA). The ACA now represents nearly 60,000 professional counselors, counselor educators, and other human development specialists in 16 national specialty divisions, with 4 regional assemblies and 56 state branches. In addition to its far-reaching efforts to meet the professional needs of counselors, the ACA has also involved itself in other areas that demonstrate the maturity of the profession as a whole. The first is the development, refinement, and expansion of

---

[1] Other certification bodies include the Commission on Rehabilitation Counselor Certification and the National Academy for Certified Family Therapists. The National Board for Certified Counselors includes the National Certified Career Counselors (NCCC), the National Certified Gerontological Counselors (NCGC), the National Certified School Counselors (NCSC), the Certified Clinical Mental Health Counselors (CCMHC), and the Master Addiction Counselors (MAC).

the professional code of ethics and standards of practice by which to judge the conduct of counselors and the establishment of a structure for disciplining members who violate those standards (see Appendix A). A formal procedure for receiving complaints of member misconduct, for conducting impartial hearings and appeals, and for imposing appropriate discipline has been developed and implemented through ACA's Ethics Committee. This voluntary self-regulation by members is widely heralded as a hallmark of an active, mature profession.

Another hallmark is the establishment of a legal defense fund that, in appropriate circumstances, provides limited funds or *amicus curiae* ("friend of the court") briefs to support counselors who are defending a lawsuit. This, too, has been refined and expanded and is now known as the ACA Legal Action Program. The ACA Insurance Trust was established in 1966 to provide professional liability coverage for counselors and students in counseling (see Appendix B). Subscribers are entitled to call the Trust's Risk Management Hotline with practice management and other questions to avoid potential liability. Finally, ACA committees and related corporate entities have been created to respond to various external and internal changes in the counseling profession in the areas of licensure, credentialing, accreditation of training programs, government, and public relations, to name a few.

What all this means to a counselor faced with any of a wide variety of legal entanglements is this: Counseling is largely viewed today as a mature, diversified profession with established standards governing the professional conduct of its members. As a result, the conduct of counseling professionals is scrutinized both from within and without the profession against these established standards for preparation, competence, conduct, and most important, for the care provided to clients.

CHAPTER 2

OVERVIEW OF
LAW AND ETHICS

At the close of the 20th century virtually every aspect of American society is affected by the all-pervasiveness of the law. Employment, community involvement and activities, leisure opportunities, and even family relationships are legislated and regulated. Counselors also deal with all these facets of life and are subject to a variety of legal and ethical considerations governing their professional practice. It is critical that counselors understand the basic concepts of the legal system, the general body of law affecting professional practice, and the impact of professional conduct and ethical standards to be prepared to address potential problems as they arise in practice.

Legal issues are to be distinguished from ethical considerations and standards of practice developed by the profession that should be applied in professional practice. This chapter is designed to help counselors understand and appreciate the differences and relationships between the two types of requirements.

The American Legal Structure

The American legal system as we know it today evolved from the common law system of England. Our ancestors brought with them from England a detailed code of regulations to govern behavior that formed the basis for law in the New World. Americans also are governed by the U.S. Constitution, which established our tripartite form of government to initiate, administer, and enforce laws passed by the Congress of the United States (federal laws) and the several states.

Within this structure, laws governing our society derive from two sources: laws passed by governmental bodies such as the Congress or state legislatures, and "rules of law" made by the courts in interpreting the Constitution, federal and state law, and the common law. Law made by courts, sometimes called *judge-made law*, takes into account the relevant facts of each particular case, the applicable statutes and administrative regulations governing the situation, and decisions from other court cases (called *precedents*) that might bear on the facts of the case before the court. This all-inclusive approach to interpreting individual cases results in an ever-evolving body of law, within the overall framework of the Constitution, that reflects the changing character of our society.

In appropriate cases courts also consider standards of conduct relevant to a particular profession, as mentioned in Chapter 1. Taking the customary conduct of similarly situated professionals into account when interpreting the particular facts of a case has been an important safeguard for both the public and the affected professionals in many cases.

This all boils down to the concept that our body of laws is dynamic and ever-changing. It is not possible to predict accurately the result of any particular case that might be presented in the future, but rules of law guide the analysis of situations that may develop. It is those general rules of law that we attempt to present in the remaining chapters.

Civil and Criminal Law

There are two distinct types of law: criminal law and civil law. Basically, criminal, or penal law, includes acts that are prosecuted by the government, not private individuals. Crimes are punishable by fine, imprisonment, or death, and include offenses such as murder, rape, theft, robbery, assault with a deadly weapon, abuse, and the like. Individuals can also be prosecuted for aiding and abetting someone who has committed such crimes, or for failing to notify proper authorities in some situations when they have knowledge of such crimes.

Civil law generally includes everything that is not criminal in nature concerning the civil rights of individuals or other bodies. Violations of civil laws are enforced by private persons bringing suit against the violators in a court of law. The sanctions awarded to successful plaintiffs are usually in the form of monetary damages to compensate the plaintiff for his or her loss. Most of the legal issues involving counselors fall into this category.

The Court System

Federal Courts

Federal courts were created by Article III, §2, of the Constitution of the United States and have the power to hear cases "arising under this Constitution" and the laws of the United States. Federal law provides for two situations where cases may be brought in federal courts. The first is where the case arises under the laws of the United States or presents a question of federal law (federal question jurisdiction, 28 U.S.C. §1331). The second is where the case involves citizens of different states and the amount in controversy exceeds $50,000 (diversity jurisdiction, 28 U.S.C. §1332). These are the only types of cases that may be heard in federal courts, and the limitation is important. Potential litigants have the option to bring their claims in either state or federal court if the jurisdictional requirements of the federal system can be met.

State Courts

Most state courts are patterned after the federal system, with trial courts, a middle-level appellate court, and a supreme court as the final arbiter of decisions involving state and federal laws that affect the residents of the state. The names of these courts may vary from state to state, but their function is essentially the same. They can hear both civil and criminal cases arising under either state or federal laws, and their decisions are binding on the residents of the state unless overturned by a higher court within the state or by a federal court.

Appellate Process

In both the state and federal court systems, cases originate in the trial court (called the Federal District Court in the federal system). Both parties put on their case at this level, witnesses are heard, evidence is taken, the relevant law is applied to the facts, and a decision is rendered either by a judge or by a jury. Finally, the judge assigns the appropriate remedies to the parties.

Parties may have the right to appeal decisions of the trial or district court to the intermediate-level appeals court. In the federal system, these 13 courts are called the U.S. Circuit Courts of Appeals. Their function is to review how the law has been applied to the facts of each particular case and to determine whether the trial court made any errors in its decision that should be overturned, reversed, or sent

7

back to the trial court for additional findings of fact. The state appeals courts generally operate in a similar manner.

Finally, losing parties can request that their case be heard at the third and final level: either the highest court in the state system or in the federal system, the U.S. Supreme Court. In addition, cases that have been decided by the highest Court of a state may move to the U.S. Supreme Court through the process known as the *petition for certiorari*, or asking the Court to hear the case. The nine justices of the Supreme Court then vote to decide whether to hear the case, and, if at least four justices agree, the Court will issue a *writ of certiorari* asking that the case be forwarded to the Supreme Court. Cases accepted by the Supreme Court generally involve issues of federal law where decisions of circuit courts on similar issues conflict with one another.

Ethical Standards

In addition to the legal considerations that govern the conduct of all citizens, counselors also are guided in their professional conduct by the ethical standards promulgated by professional associations, such as the *ACA Code of Ethics and Standards of Practice* (1995); (see Appendix A). According to Huey and Remley (1988), these standards illustrate for counselors "the behaviors to which they should aspire and give general guidelines for addressing difficult issues" (p.1). Reviewed and revised periodically, the standards provide a comprehensive source of authority to advise counselors in their daily practice. As set out in the preamble to the *ACA Code of Ethics*, "the specification of a code of ethics enables the association to clarify to current and future members, and to those served by members, the nature of the ethical responsibilities held in common by its members."

Ethical standards also serve as the basis for processing complaints against members of an association and are enforced internally through the Ethics Committee of the ACA. A complaint procedure has been established and penalties for violations of the standards have been set, which may include oral or written reprimands, probation, suspension or termination of membership, or revocation of credentials.

Ethical decisions generally complement the legal parameters but also cover issues that tend to fall into the grey areas, not expressly prohibited, yet not specifically allowed by the law. They take into account the subtle variations of facts in each situation and the reasonable approach to addressing it. The concept of what is ethical also changes with the maturity and perspective of the counseling profession and society at large. For example, as information technology plays a larger role in practice, questions concerning its impact on client confidentiality arise as well. There are no clear answers to all the specific issues as yet, but it is likely that in the future the *ACA Code of Ethics* will address a variety of topics we cannot yet even imagine.

Occasionally ethical standards and responsibilities conflict with legal standards and requirements. Probably the most common example of this involves the ethical requirement to maintain client confidences in the face of a court order to reveal that information. The counselor may certainly request to be excused based on the need to protect client confidences, but, if the court continues to require the counselor to testify, he or she must comply. The discussions in Chapter 4 explain this issue in greater detail.

Together with the 1995 revisions to the *Code of Ethics*, the ACA has published *Standards of Practice* (Appendix A) that set out the minimum behavioral statements of the *Code of Ethics*. ACA has also published the *ACA Ethical Standards Casebook*, Fifth Edition (1996), to provide specific examples to illustrate and clarify the meaning and intent of each of the standards. Freshly revised, the book presents typical situations a counselor may face in practice and analyzes the ethical considerations involved in each situation. Counselors are well advised to study the implications of these analyses carefully and to apply the results to their personal practices.

Ethics and the Law

The ethical standards of a profession are generally enforced through the internal procedures of the professional association, not specifically by courts of law. Yet, in the absence of any clear statutory authority or case law precedent to guide a court in a case involving the conduct of an individual counselor, courts may apply the standard of care given by other similarly situated professionals, in this case other counselors. Courts may also look to the self-imposed standards of the profession to determine liability. Thus counselors should act in accordance with the standards of counselors in their local community and thoroughly study and follow the *ACA Code of Ethics and Standards of Practice* where they apply as a means of avoiding potential liability. Just as courts have utilized the ethical guidelines and standards of care developed by the legal, accounting, and medical professions, a court could find that a counselor has breached his or her professional duty to a client on the basis of the counseling profession's own internal ethical standards.

9

CHAPTER 3

THE COUNSELING
RELATIONSHIP

A successful counseling relationship demands that the client have unquestioned confidence and trust in the counselor. That aspect of this unique relationship creates a duty to act in the client's best interest, using the counselor's skills and training to benefit the client. This is the basis of any *fiduciary relationship*. As a result of this fiduciary duty, the professional counselor is expected to meet established standards of professional competence and preparation, respect the standards of conduct in professional practice, and exercise a certain level of care in dealing with clients called *due care*. For some professional relationships, such as those between lawyers and clients or doctors and patients, a large body of law has produced a fairly accurate definition of exactly what those standards might include. Although there is not a large collection of pertinent decisions defining the fiduciary duty owed to clients by professional counselors, there are established standards of conduct and ethical guidelines to follow. In states where the conduct of professional counselors is regulated by certification, licensure, or registration statutes there are administrative guidelines and rules. Courts also draw on existing law as it applies to other professions and relate that law to the counseling situation when appropriate. As a result, some of the cases cited in this book involve psychiatrists or psychologists, as well as other mental health counselors, because the factual situations could occur in any counseling relationship.

Counselors also have *contractual* duties arising from their relationships with clients. A contract is a legal relationship, either written or oral, created by an agreement between the parties. This relationship can be expressly stated, as in a private practice setting where the client comes to the counselor's office regularly, has a written service plan and fee agreement, and pays fees for professional services rendered. Alternatively, a contract may be implied from the circumstances of the relationship between the parties, even though no fees may be charged.

It is important to know at what point the fiduciary and contractual obligations of counselors come into existence and these obligations should be determined by the start of the professional counseling relationship. When does an individual become a "client?"

Who Is a Client?

Once an individual walks through the door of the counselors' office the counselor must set the tone of discussions and determine at what point that person becomes a client. First and foremost should come an exchange of information. A "screening" on both sides is needed to determine the nature of information or assistance requested by the potential client (intake information) and whether the counselor has the training, experience, competence, and legal authority to render treatment. Referral to another professional may be appropriate at this point if, in the professional judgment of the counselor, the needs of the potential client are outside the competency or scope of practice of the counselor.

The discussion should also include the counselor's professional identity and treatment methodology, circumstances of treatment, client rights and responsibilities, expectations of outcome, risks associated with treatment or refusing treatment, and possible alternatives. The counselor also should initiate a discussion of the business arrangements for fees, insurance claims, appointments and cancellation policies, and the like. Finally, procedures for termination of counseling should be discussed. This information will enable both sides to decide whether or not to enter into a counseling relationship and will establish the basis for *informed consent*.

Consent to Treatment

One of the most widely recognized means of initiating the trust and understanding necessary in a counseling relationship is to secure the *informed consent* to treat the client. This process, and the written document that should come from it, according to Bertram and Wheeler (1994), is designed to "define the basic treatment relationship between counselor and client. Misunderstanding and disappointment, which is often the genesis of a liability claim, can be reduced when clients are made knowledgeable of the ground rules of the counseling relationship" (p. 15).

The duty to obtain the informed consent of clients has largely developed from case law imposed on the medical profession, although the 1995 revisions to the *ACA Code of Ethics and Standards of Practice* (Appendix A) contain several passages devoted to client rights and informed consent. Generally, clients must be *competent* to give their *voluntary consent* based on sufficient *knowledge* of the counseling relationship to understand what they are consenting to. *Competence* for this purpose means the client is able to understand the nature of the procedure or course of treatment, the possible risks and benefits, and any other information relevant to treatment, such as confidentiality, fees, timing, counseling approach, and credentials of the counselor. To ensure that consent to treatment is *voluntary*, the client must be free from undue influence or coercion. Finally, accurate and complete information must be provided the client so a reasoned, informed consent can be given. Such consent must be obtained from a parent or guardian for a client who is a minor or is incompetent to give that consent.

The process of providing and securing informed consent from a client may be oral or written, but some written expression of the client's consent should be acquired and maintained with the counselor's records. No comprehensive document provides the necessary information or agreed-upon form memorializing the agreement, but Bertram and Wheeler (1994) prepared a good checklist of the information to be included in informed written consent for treatment (Appendix C). Crawford (1994) also recommends that the client add a statement in his or her own handwriting at the conclusion of the typed or printed version to accentuate the fact that the client has *read and understands* the information and gives his or her consent freely.

Because the process of providing information and securing consent forms the basis of the relationship between the counselor and the client, it is important to prepare the material carefully in advance to avoid any omissions or confusion of information, rights, and responsibilities. Counselors must also understand when in the course of a relationship additional information is necessary to reflect the changing direction of treatment and be sure to secure informed consent at that point, as well. Pretreatment guidelines and careful monitoring during treatment will help clients develop more realistic expectations of the counseling process and could head off claims against the counselor based on misunderstandings.

13

Monitoring and Terminating Relationships

Counselors have an obligation to monitor the ongoing relationship with each client to determine when changes in treatment, new information, the client's status or perception of treatment or progress occur and to secure informed consent as necessary. Consistently missing appointments, falling behind in payments, failure to complete counseling assignments, or other variations in the behavior of a client could be an indication of problems with the counseling relationship itself and need to be managed in a timely way.

Documenting client records regularly is an ongoing obligation for counselors. Although there is no rule about how this should be accomplished, a reasonable standard of care must be exercised in preparing and maintaining client records during the relationship and can help a counselor avoid liability at some future time.

When the ground rules for the counseling relationship and for termination are clearly laid out in the initial process of securing informed consent, the process of termination should not come as a shock to the client. Counselors need to exercise care in preparing a client for termination, and an established set of procedures makes the transition much easier. This should include providing notice, respecting the clients' right to terminate, making appropriate referrals when this is a prudent course, attending to the clients' anxiety or concerns about the future, and bringing closure to the professional relationship. Also important is to plan ahead for your own business needs, such as requesting final payments for services and discussing how to dispose of counseling records.

Counselors are well advised to request that clients keep current on fees owed for services or terminate the relationship if appropriate. This also applies to fees for the final counseling session, although collecting on a final payment may be difficult, and perhaps unwise. As Crawford (1994) noted, "persistent attempts to collect a last payment from a client, however justified, seem to invite legal or ethical complaints" (p. 67).

Fees for Service

You have prepared long and hard to achieve a level of professional competence, secured the requisite credentials, become licensed or registered to practice in your state, affiliated with other professionals in your area, joined your national, state, and specialty professional associations, and hung out your shingle to practice. You are entitled to charge $75 or $80 or more for each counseling session, right? Perhaps. The amount of fees, if any, a professional counselor is entitled to charge will depend on a variety of circumstances, including the financial status of the clients, the customary charges for such services in the locality, the level of expertise or specialty of the practice, and the employment situation of the counselor. The *ACA Code of Ethics and Standards of Practice* advise counselors to discuss fee arrangements and collection procedures with clients prior to entering the counseling relationship. Counselors are instructed to consider the financial status of clients and locality in setting fees and to attempt to find comparable services of acceptable cost for a client if the counselor's fees are inappropriate for the client (see section A.10.b of the code in Appendix A).

Counselors employed in agencies or institutions may be prohibited by agency regulation from accepting fees for services, including services provided outside the institution in their private practices in some cases involving agency clients. In addition, according to the *ACA Code of Ethics*, professional "counselors do not accept a referral fee from other professionals" (D.3.b.).

Regardless of the amount of fees charged, counselors should have clear fee arrangements with clients, preferably in writing, that specify the amount of fees per counseling session, how fees will be assessed for missed appointments, terms for payment (at time service is rendered, within 30 days, etc.), and any special charges that may apply for reports, evaluations, interest charged on overdue accounts, and the like. Insurance claims and reimbursement procedures should also be specified. A written fee agreement puts clients on notice that the professional services are a serious obligation that must be fulfilled.

Even with a written agreement, some clients will fall behind on payments and the counselor must take steps to encourage the client to pay on overdue accounts. Do not allow your clients to become seriously delinquent in payments, and do not agree to "write off" fees for services after the fact. Counselors can pursue legal claims against clients in small claims or other courts but should be cautioned that attempting to collect on overdue fees can push clients to file claims against the counselor. Probably the best course of action is to meet with the client and openly and honestly discuss the outstanding debt, with a view to encouraging responsibility and prompt payment. Counselors are not obligated to continue services to a nonpaying client indefinitely, but should take steps to refer the client to another therapist or counseling service to avoid an accusation of abandonment. As with all difficult situations, be sure to document your files thoroughly with complete information on the past due account, your attempts to invite payment, and your chosen course of action.

Dual Relationships

Dual relationships, where a mental health professional stands in two or more roles with a person who has sought his or her help, affect virtually all counselors in all practice settings. The resulting role conflicts and ethical dilemmas can and do lead to ethical and licensing complaints or legal liability. Rarely are such relationships a clear-cut matter because the specific facts of the situation vary so widely. Can you accept a social invitation from a student? A supervisor? Should you collaborate on a research paper with a client? What if that paper focuses on some aspect of the counseling relationship? Where boundaries should be drawn is sometimes difficult to establish. Such dilemmas resulted in numerous inquiries to the ACA Ethics Committee during 1993–1994 (Garcia, Glosoff, & Smith, 1994).

Dual relationships, according to Herlihy and Corey (1992), "can be problematic along a number of dimensions: (1) they are pervasive; (2) they can be difficult to recognize; (3) they are sometimes unavoidable; (4) they can be very harmful but are not always harmful; and (5) they are the subject of conflicting advice from expert sources" (p. 7). Most agree that dual relationships tend to harm the counseling process in a variety of unintended ways. Clients may feel they are being manipulated or exploited in their nonprofessional collaboration because of their reliance on the counselor in the counseling side of their relationship. The counselor may experience a loss of objectivity in the counseling relationship because of the noncounseling association. Both parties may find it difficult to separate the two relationships and the information gained in each. This confusion can lead to further misunderstandings and to real or perceived breaches of confidentiality.

The *ACA Code of Ethics* cautions professional counselors to avoid dual relationships when possible (A.6.a.) because of the potential for impaired professional judgment and increased risk of harm to their clients. Where such relationships cannot be avoided, however, counselors are to "take appropriate professional precautions such as informed consent, consultation, supervision, and documentation to ensure that judgment is not impaired and no exploitation occurs" (A.6.a). Further, counselor educators and trainers need to "clearly define and maintain ethical, professional, and social relationship boundaries with their students and supervisees." Further, they must "explain to students and supervisees the potential for the relationship to become exploitative" (F.1.b.). These ethical statements are important because whenever there is a potential of harm to a client, student or supervisee, the standard of practice will hold the counselor responsible for managing the risk of harm through appropriate safeguards.

Should the counselor find herself in a dual relationship, Bertram and Wheeler (1994) note, the first step is to determine whether it is avoidable or unavoidable. Most dual relationships can be avoided. Second, assess the possible risks and benefits of the nonprofessional association. Seek an objective opinion from a trusted colleague. If you decide that the second relationship is avoidable or might jeopardize your legal and ethical responsibilities to your client, you should decline the second relationship. You may also need to help the client find assistance elsewhere. If you decide to continue the secondary relationship, work with your client to define the boundaries of both relationships. Have an honest conversation about the risks involved and your ability to remain objective. Be sure to document your discussions in the client's chart and obtain a written consent to treatment that acknowledges the two relationships. Finally, a prudent counselor will also engage in regular supervision to be sure the dual relationship remains untainted.

Most mental health professionals readily acknowledge that sexual intimacies with a client are not only unethical but also probably illegal. Yet from 1987 to 1992, data compiled by the ACA Insurance Trust, Inc. (Nelson, 1995b), shows that approximately 13% of all liability actions brought against counselors were based on claims of sexual misconduct. In many states such relationships are illegal as well, and the consequences range from ethical sanctions and license revocation to civil suits and criminal prosecution. Counselors also must take care to distinguish between appropriate and inappropriate touching of a client or student and recognize that even a seemingly innocent hug can form the basis of a complaint.

Consultation With Colleagues

With so many opportunities to violate ethical or legal boundaries arising in the day-to-day practice of counseling, let alone the variety of substantive questions that arise in helping to resolve specific client issues, it is often difficult to know for certain how to proceed. Consultation with other qualified professional counselors thus becomes significant in making reasoned standard-of-care decisions and in attempting to avoid claims of counselor malpractice. Certainly a mentor or consultant could corroborate or support you in the event that becomes necessary.

Counselors should identify mentors, consultants, or supervisors who can provide guidance in routine matters and when they have doubts as to whether a course of conduct might violate the *ACA Code of Ethics*. A working relationship should be established in advance of the need to do so, including the "ground rules" for your consultation. These would include an understanding of the nature of the assistance to be given and received, and the resulting level of responsibility. Is the relationship direct supervision (as distinguished from clinical supervision), consultation, informal advice, or merely casual conversation? How will you ensure that the communications between you are adequate to give a complete picture of the issues under consideration? Are the consultant's (or counselor's) internal procedures sufficient to ensure confidentiality as information is shared? Who will document the consultation, and how extensively? If you are asked to consult, how do you ensure that the counselor requesting your assistance is competent and qualified?

The *ACA Code of Ethics* cautions that

> Information obtained in a consulting relationship is discussed for professional purposes only with persons clearly concerned with the case. Written and oral reports present data germane to the purposes of the consultation, and every effort is made to protect client identity and avoid undue invasion of privacy (B.6.a.).

It is important that support staff also understand the need to keep client information confidential.

CHAPTER 4

PROTECTING
CLIENT CONFIDENCES

I t is widely recognized that the effectiveness of the relationship between counselor and client hinges on a fulcrum of trust. Unless the client has complete trust in the counselor, it is unlikely that information can be freely exchanged, and the purpose of the relationship will be frustrated. Complete trust can be established only if the client believes that his or her communications with the counselor will remain *confidential*. Counselors and all mental health professionals have a clear ethical duty to respect each client's right to privacy and to protect information obtained from their clients from unwarranted disclosure (see Section B of the *ACA Code of Ethics* in Appendix A).

There is also a legal duty to protect client confidences in many states that arises in the context of a court or administrative proceeding. Where the confidential nature of a professional–client relationship is expressly recognized by statute or by common law, information obtained through that relationship is called *privileged communication*, and the professional will not be compelled by a court or administrative body to reveal that information.

Even though only about 10% of the claims made against counselors in recent years have arisen from confidentiality issues, it is clear that the area still causes confusion and concern for many counselors. The ACA Insurance Trust, Inc., Risk Management Service reports that between January 1993 and March 1994 there were 169 inquiries on the issue, including requests for advice on subpoenas (Nelson, 1995b). It is important that counselors understand the development of the twin concepts of confidentiality and privileged communication, their applicability in practice, and the limits of each.

Common Law Beginnings

The concept originated in the early English common law when it became obvious that clients would not talk freely to their lawyers if they feared their secrets might be revealed in a criminal trial when their lawyers were forced to testify. To promote free exchange of information in this situation, an exception to the rule was carved out prohibiting lawyers from revealing their clients' confidences in court testimony. This privilege was later extended to the husband-wife relationship in the interest of preserving family harmony. No privilege was recognized in early common law for communications between physicians and their patients or between priests and penitents, but they are now sanctioned by state law in many American jurisdictions.

Privileged Communication

Although ethical practice dictates that client confidences not be revealed, except in limited circumstances, professional–client confidentiality is recognized in the context of raising a "privilege" against revealing information that was disclosed by a client in confidence. *This occurs only when the professional is called as a witness in a court of law.* For the privilege to apply, the communication must have been made *in confidence, with the indicated desire that it remain so.* This desire need not be explicitly stated, however; a simple action such as closing the office door so that a conversation can remain private indicates the desire for secrecy. *The communication generally must not be made in the presence or hearing of third persons* if it is to be judged confidential. The exception to this is if there is some confidential relationship involving the third person as well, for example an interpreter, spouse, parent, or perhaps another employee or counselor who is involved with the client.

Over the years the rule of privilege has been narrowly extended to cover other relationships, but has been recognized by courts only when expressly provided by common law or state statute. In the absence of state statute, some flexibility is allowed courts in determining whether to recognize the privilege against disclosing confidences based on a balancing of interests test. Courts analyze whether the public policy of requiring every person to testify to all facts inquired into by a court of law is outweighed by the competing public interest in the particular relationship sought to be protected. Four criteria are generally recognized in determining whether the privilege should be granted:

1. The communications must originate in *confidence* that they will not be disclosed.
2. This element of *confidentiality must be essential* to the full and satisfactory maintenance of the relationship between the parties.
3. The *relation* must be one in which in the opinion of the community ought to be sedulously *fostered*.
4. The *injury* that would inure to the relation by the disclosure of the communications must be *greater than the benefit* thereby gained for the correct disposal of litigation (Wigmore, 1961, emphasis in original).

Only if all four of these criteria are present should the privilege be granted. Although the courts generally recognize and apply these criteria in cases presented before them,[1] judges are reluctant to expand the privileges in the absence of state legislation. Thus in states where the counselor-client relationship is not expressly recognized by statute as privileged, a counselor could be required to testify concerning information received from a client. It should be noted that the counselor's own thoughts and impressions may still be protected, however, as discussed under Reports and Records in this chapter.

Federal courts have more flexibility in recognizing privileged communications within the scope of the Federal Rules of Evidence and Criminal Procedure. In the absence of state law to the contrary, federal courts may apply the privilege "in the light of reason and experience" (Rule 501, Federal Rules of Evidence). State courts with similar procedures may also have wider latitude in extending privileges beyond what is expressly recognized by statute.

The United States Circuit Courts of Appeals are divided on this issue. The Second and Sixth Circuits determined that "reason and experience" compel recognition of the psychotherapist-patient privilege in both civil and criminal cases (*In re Doe*, 1992, and *In re Zuniga*, 1983). The Fifth, Ninth, Tenth, and Eleventh Circuits, however, in criminal proceedings interpreted Rule 501 as limiting the development of privileges to those recognized by common law (*United States v. Burtrum*, 1994; *In re Grand Jury Proceedings*, 1989; *United States v. Corona*, 1988; *United States v. Meagher*, 1976).

The Seventh Circuit weighed in for recognition of the privilege in *Jaffee v. Redmond* (1995). In this case a policewoman sought counsel-

---

[1] For a recent case using this analysis, see United States v. Friedman, 636 F. Supp. 462 (S.D.N.Y. 1986).

ing from a licensed and certified clinical social worker employed by the village after fatally shooting a suspect. The family of the deceased suspect sued the police officer, the department, and the village, alleging use of deadly force in violation of the suspect's civil rights. In the course of discovery before the trial, the plaintiffs learned the policewoman had been in counseling and sought to compel the social worker to testify at the trial and to turn over her notes and records on her sessions with the policewoman.

The trial court ruled that there is no privilege between a social worker and client, but the policewoman refused to grant a waiver of her rights and the social worker refused to reveal the substance of the counseling sessions. As a result, the judge told jurors that they could assume the information withheld would have been unfavorable to the policewoman, and the jury awarded $545,000 to the suspect's family.

The Seventh Circuit reversed the trial judge on the issue of the jury instruction and recognized that there are compelling arguments for recognizing communications between psychotherapists and patients as privileged. According to the court,

> Much has changed with the mental health field in the past five years. The need, and demand, for counseling services has skyrocketed during the past several years due to the rapid spread of violence and crime throughout our nation. Countless innocent bystanders, as well as law enforcement officers themselves, witness violent crimes and homicides. These unfortunate individuals, who include not only law enforcement personnel, but also students, school and hospital employees, postal workers, and members of the general public, need and deserve the help, support, and emotional release provided by confidential counseling. The recognition of a psychotherapist/patient privilege can serve to encourage troubled individuals, as well as those who witness, participate in, and are intimately affected by acts of violence in today's stressful, crime ridden, homicidal environment, to seek the necessary professional counseling and to assist mental health professionals to succeed in their endeavors (p. 1355).

The court also concluded that psychotherapists and patients share a unique relationship that depends on the freedom to communicate openly, relying on the varying forms of the privilege already recognized by all state statutes. In fact, the 1994 statute in Illinois, where the case arose, specifically extends the privilege to therapists, including psychiatrists, physicians, psychologists, social workers, or nurses who provide mental health or development disabilities services. As a result, the court ruled that the confidential communications between the policewoman and the social worker were protected from disclosure.

The Supreme Court granted certiorari to hear this case to resolve the conflict between the circuits in October 1995. Arguments should be heard in the case in early 1996, and a decision is expected by the summer of 1996. Whether this will resolve the issue of communications between professional counselors who do not specifically fit into the state statutory definition (as in Illinois) is yet to be seen.

Thus there are two schools of thought concerning the extension of the privilege not to reveal confidences to the counselor-client relationship. On one hand, the judiciary probably has the discretion, as we have seen from the cases, to appraise the relationship, to determine that it meets the four criteria set out by Dean Wigmore as the basis for a confidential relationship, and to rule that communications within such a relationship are to remain confidential. Others believe that this expansion can come only through legislative action, and those who want to ensure the confidentiality of the counseling relationship must look to state legislatures. Many states have taken the initiative and enacted statutes that guarantee confidentiality in several counseling relationships. Counselors are urged to determine the scope of privileged communications in the state(s) in which they practice and to advise their clients accordingly.

Given this diversity of thought on the question of confidentiality in the counseling relationship, what should a counselor tell a client who says, "I have a problem I'd like to discuss with you; will you keep it strictly confidential?" The answer depends on a number of things. In the vast majority of counseling situations, no information will ever be revealed to the counselor that could become important in a court of law. There need be no restriction to a client, for example, in disclosing incidents relating to self-development. *Counselors have the obligation to keep all information relating to the counseling relationship confidential, except when required to testify or provide information to a court of law*, or in the limited situations described later.

In initial disclosure discussions with clients, counselors should inform clients of their right to expect confidentiality and the limits counselors face, including the possibility of court-compelled testimony, consultation with other counseling professionals or supervisors, and the duty to warn exceptions discussed later in this chapter. Counselors can tell clients that they are bound by the *ACA Code of Ethics*, which states that "counselors should respect their clients' right to privacy and avoid illegal and unwarranted disclosures of confidential information" (B.1.a.). They should understand that you will share information only with other professionals who are clearly concerned with the case and will make every effort "to protect client identity and avoid undue invasion of privacy" (B.6.a.).

Finally, if called to testify in court in a state that does not expressly recognize the counselor-client privilege, the counselor can and should apprise the court of the fact that he or she is a licensed (or certified or registered) professional counselor, bound by a code of ethics that requires respect for the client's right to privacy, and that testifying would violate professional obligations. A ruling from the court on the applicability of the privilege in this situation should be requested and followed.

Whose Privilege Is It?

Both the legal privilege not to reveal information and the right of confidentiality belong to the client, and the professional counselor has the duty to protect those client rights. On the other hand, the client may choose to _waive_ the privilege and reveal information on his or her own and can authorize disclosure of any confidential material to anyone. A counselor is obligated to disclose information when requested to do so by the client, but only information that is specifically requested, and only to the individuals or agencies specified by the client. Many counselors request written authorization from clients before they will provide information, for example, to insurance companies, and keep these written waivers in the clients' files. Even in jurisdictions where this is not a legal requirement, it is a good practice to protect the counselor if a question regarding permission arises later. Counselors, like other professionals, may be held liable for the _unauthorized disclosure_ of confidential client information.

Arthur and Swanson (1993) pointed out other situations in the day-to-day management of the counseling practice that should be discussed with clients. Clients should understand, for example, if a counselor is receiving systematic clinical supervision and what that means to the client's right to privacy. Further, clients should understand that clerical assistants and other employees may process information and materials relating to the client and have access to records for billing and record keeping. Counselors should advise clients of the ethical mandate to obtain professional consultation, and clients should be given the names of any colleagues consulted if information identifying a client is revealed. Underage clients should understand that their parents or guardians (in some states) may have a legal right to know of the communications between the counselor and minor. Finally, clients have a right to know when sharing of confidential information is part of the treatment process in an agency or institution, or if it is mandatory, in the case of a penal system.

In addition to the voluntary authorization to waive the right to privacy, clients may waive the legal privilege of confidentiality by their actions. If they voluntarily communicate the same information to a colleague, roommate, or friend, for example, or if a disinterested third party is in the room when the information is divulged, the privilege may be lost.

There also are situations where the privilege does not apply to client communications. This includes incidents where the client initiates an action against the counselor before a state agency, such as a licensing board, or in a malpractice lawsuit. The client has, in effect, waived the privilege in these cases by putting his or her *own* condition in issue in the case. Along this same line, a defendant who claims insanity as a defense in a criminal case cannot also claim the physician-patient or counselor-client privilege and withhold evidence of his or her condition, because it is relevant to the defense of insanity. In a custody suit, a parent who raises the issue of mental health may also be authorizing the release of the counselor's records. Similarly counselors are not proscribed from taking appropriate actions to protect themselves when their client's conduct poses a danger to them. If a client is threatening, harassing, or stalking a counselor, the counselor needs to seek protection.

Limits of the Privilege

It is important to remember that one of the primary duties of a professional counselor is to protect the client and others from harm. As a result of that duty, and the competing interests of society in safety and security, there are several counseling situations where the ethical and legal confidentiality requirements do not apply to the same extent, if at all. In fact, in some cases the counselor has an affirmative obligation to report information learned through the counseling relationship to appropriate authorities.

Duty to Report

There are situations where the public interest in disclosing client confidences outweighs the rights of clients to keep communications privileged. This is another category of tremendous confusion for counselors, as evidenced by the number of inquiries to the ACA Insurance Trust's Risk Management Service. When a counselor determines that a clear and imminent danger exists to a client or some third person, for example, the counselor clearly has an *ethical obligation* (B.1.c.) to disclose that information, even if it is otherwise confidential, to the proper authorities. The counselor may also have a *legal duty* to notify proper authorities and potential victims in certain cases. For example, virtually all states now require reporting incidents of child abuse, and reporting of spousal, elder, and disabled adult abuse is permitted or required in some states. In all such cases protecting potential or actual victims, who may not be in a position to report the abuse themselves, outweighs the client's right to keep the information confidential. Reporting past incidents of child, elder, and disabled adult abuse also may be required in some states. In these cases the counselor-client privilege does not apply and there may be significant penalties if the counselor fails to report the abuse or neglect. In *Searcy v. Auerbach* (1992), the Ninth Circuit Court of Appeals ruled that a psychologist who did not follow statutory procedures for reporting child abuse was not immune from civil liability. The psychologist not only failed to make the required report, but he also disclosed his opinion to the child's father, who was not authorized to receive that information under the reporting statute.

In addition to mandatory or permissive reporting of abuse cases, the counselor may also have a duty to warn potential victims of abuse in cases where a client threatens harm. Counselors should take care to follow the guidelines for duty to warn discussed in this chapter.

It is more difficult to draw the line in revealing client information when the risk of harm is great, but not necessarily imminent. Recent attention has focused on reporting drug or alcohol abuse, particularly where abusers continue to drive automobiles or operate heavy machinery while under the influence of such substances. More subtle cases involve clients who take prescription medications or who suffer from some mental disease or condition that impairs their ability to drive safely.

Counselors should consider steps to protect the public from imminent danger in all these cases. Once a counselor knows or should have known that a client poses a danger to others, the duty to protect arises. Possible actions include convincing the client not to drive, reporting the hazard to local police or other law enforcement officials, or seeking involuntary commitment when appropriate.

Whether there is also a corresponding duty to warn possible victims of clients known to be unsafe drivers depends on state law and on whether there is a readily identifiable and foreseeable potential victim. If state law requires a communicated threat before warning is required, or if there is no foreseeable and identifiable potential victim, a counselor may be precluded from taking further steps in this situation other than reporting to local authorities or seeking commitment if appropriate. However, the Wisconsin Supreme Court ruled that a jury might find that family members of a mentally impaired patient are foreseeable victims of her dangerous driving. If the treating psychiatrist failed to commit his patient or warn of the dangerous side effects of her medication on her ability to drive, according to the court, an accident could be found to be the result of his negligent treatment. Similarly the court ruled that, "if it is ultimately proven that it would have been foreseeable to a psychiatrist, exercising due care, that by failing to warn a third person or by failing to institute detention or commitment proceedings someone would be harmed, negligence will be established" (*Schuster v. Altenberg,* 1988). Therefore the psychiatrist in this case should have warned the family of his patient's condition and of the potential side effects of the medication.

Another difficult area to consider involves warning partners of HIV-positive clients. Knowing the potential for transmission of HIV and the deadly nature of the resulting AIDS infection, society certainly has an interest in protecting unsuspecting partners of clients who may be HIV-positive, even in the absence of a legal requirement to do so. All states now have statutory guidelines for reporting HIV-positive cases and maintaining confidentiality, although most are limited to reporting by physicians. Warning spouses, known sexual partners, and other individuals with whom an HIV-positive patient shares needles is also permitted by physicians in most states, and a counselor, too, may have an obligation to warn endangered third parties.

But what about the client's competing right to privacy? The *ACA Code of Ethics* (B.1.d.) does not require counselors to warn an identifiable third person of the risks, but it does hold the counselor justified in disclosing the information under the same duty to warn exceptions outlined in the *Tarasoff v. Regents of the University of California* (1976) scenario described in the next section of this chapter. Before deciding to warn the third party, however, the counselor must determine that the client has not already warned the individual about the disease and does not plan to do so in the near future.

Although there is no legal or ethical requirement to report criminal activity revealed in a counseling session, a counselor may choose to do so without fear of violating confidentiality obligations in certain circumstances. This may be appropriate even where there is no imminent risk of harm. In one case, for example, a psychiatrist's anonymous call to a local crime stopper's unit was held not to violate Missouri's statutory physician-patient privilege where the psychiatrist revealed only the patient's former place of employment, knowing it would precipitate an investigation. The patient was later arrested and convicted of robbing a service station. On appeal, the Missouri Court of Appeals upheld the conviction ruling that the psychiatrist had not violated the statutory privilege that applies only to in-court testimony (*Missouri v. Beatty*, 1989).

Once again, it is imperative that counselors determine the extent of the law in the state(s) in which they practice and make a good faith effort to comply with reporting requirements.

Duty to Warn

The California Supreme Court shocked practicing therapists and counselors across the country when it ruled in 1976 that a therapist who knows or should have known that a patient poses a "serious danger of violence" and does not exercise reasonable care to protect the intended victim or notify the police can be held liable. (*Tarasoff v. Regents of the University of California*, 1976). The case involved a graduate student at the University of California–Berkeley who revealed in counseling that he intended to kill a young woman, Tatiana Tarasoff, because she had refused his advances. The psychologist considered the threat to be serious and called the campus police. They detained the student, Poddar, briefly, but released him because he seemed to be rational. They neither notified the police nor warned Tarasoff. The psychologist also reported his concerns to his supervisor, a psychiatrist, who directed that no further action be taken. Shortly thereafter Poddar murdered Tarasoff, whose parents sued the psychologist, the psychiatrist, the university counseling center, and the campus police.

The court found that certain duties and obligations arise on the part of a counselor from the "special relationship" with the client and that this "relationship may support affirmative duties for the benefit of third persons." According to the court:

> once a therapist does in fact determine, or under applicable professional standards reasonably should have determined, that a patient poses a serious danger of violence to others, he bears a duty to exercise reasonable care to protect the foreseeable victim of that danger.

But the court also noted that the confidential character of the counseling relationship is critical to its success and ought to be preserved.

> We realize that the open and confidential character of psychotherapeutic dialogue encourages patients to express threats of violence, few of which are ever executed. Certainly a therapist should not be

encouraged routinely to reveal such threats; such disclosures could seriously disrupt the patient's relationship with his therapist and with the persons threatened. To the contrary, the therapist's obligations to his patient require that he not disclose a confidence *unless such disclosure is necessary to avert danger to others,* and even then that he do so discreetly, and in a fashion that would preserve the privacy of his patient to the fullest extent compatible with the prevention of the threatened danger.

Consequently, the court concluded that the psychotherapist-patient privilege ought to be preserved, but only to the point where a competing public interest, such as preventing imminent danger to a reasonably identifiable person, intervenes. Of course, this poses a difficult call for the counselor who may have honestly misjudged a client's threats or may have made an unwarranted warning to an intended victim. The counselor might be sued for invasion of the client's right to privacy. To circumvent this, some states have enacted statutes limiting the liability of the counselor in this type of situation. To avoid potential liability, it is important to understand the limits of the *Tarasoff* court's opinion and of any subsequent decisions or legislation in your state.

Tarasoff held that liability would attach where the psychotherapist *reasonably believed, or should have believed,* that the client posed a serious danger *to an identifiable potential victim.* In the first instance, the counselor must make the judgment that the client poses a serious danger. Second, there must be an identifiable potential victim. This standard has been applied in a number of court cases,[2] and in *Davis v. Lhim* (1988), the Michigan Supreme Court enumerated factors a mental health professional should consider when deciding whether a client might act upon a threat to a third person. These include the clinical diagnosis of the patient, the context and manner in which the threat is made, the patient's opportunity to act on the threat, the patient's history of violence, the factors that provoked the threat, and whether the threats are likely to continue, the patient's response to treatment, and the patient's relationship with the potential victim.

In several cases courts have declined to impose liability in the absence of a readily identifiable victim.[3] However, the Vermont Supreme

---

[2] See, for example, McIntosh v. Milano, 403 A.2d 500 (N.J. Super. 1979); Davis v. Lhim, 335 N.W.2d 481 (Mich. Ct. App. 1988); and Eckhardt v. Kirts, 534 N.E.2d 1339 (Ill. App. Ct. 1989).

[3] See, for example, Thompson v. County of Alameda, 614 P.2d 728 (Cal. 1980); Leedy v. Hartnett, 510 F. Supp. 1125 (M.D. Pa. 1981); Brady v. Hopper,

Court ruled that a mental health professional who knows that a patient poses a risk to an identifiable person *or group* has a duty to protect that person or group from danger presented by the patient (*Peck v. Counseling Service of Addison County, Inc.*, 1985).

Other courts have held that the duty to warn extends to "foreseeable" victims of the client who may not be specifically identifiable, but nonetheless would be likely targets if the client were to become violent or carry through on threats (*Hedlund v. Superior Court*, 1983; *Jablonshi v. United States*, 1983). The Arizona Supreme Court also used this standard and found a psychiatrist liable for failing to protect a *foreseeable victim* within the "zone of danger," that is, probably at risk of harm from the patient's violent conduct (*Hamman v. County of Maricopa*, 1989).

Another court rejected the "foreseeable victim" analysis altogether, holding that there is a duty to exercise due care in determining whether a patient poses an unreasonable risk of serious bodily harm *to others* (*Perriera v. Colorado*, 1989). Yet the Florida appeals court declined to follow *Tarasoff* in 1991, ruling that imposing a duty to warn third parties would require a psychiatrist to foresee a patient's dangerousness, which is virtually impossible, and would undermine psychiatrist-patient confidentiality and trust. Florida has a statute permitting psychiatrists to warn third parties, but reporting is not mandatory (*Boynton v. Burglass*, 1991).

It is clear, however, that counselors, including school counselors, have a duty to protect clients from harming themselves, if such harm is foreseeable. In *Bogust v. Iverson* (1960), a college professor/counselor was found not responsible for the suicide of a student that occurred some 6 weeks after the counselor terminated counseling sessions with the student. The court ruled the counselor had no duty to commit, seek treatment for, or warn the parents of the student because there was no evidence that he was aware of the student's suicidal tendencies. Had such facts been alleged in this case, the results probably would have been different.

In 1991, the Maryland Court of Appeals ruled in *Eisel v. Board of Education* that summary judgment based on lack of duty to warn was not appropriate in a case where two school counselors failed to warn the parent of suicidal statements made by his child. In this case, the mother of another student reported to the counselors that Nicole Eisel

---

570 F. Supp. 1333 (D. Colo. 1983); Mavroudis v. Superior Court, 102 Cal. App. 3d 594, 162 Cal. Rptr. 724 (1980); Dunkle v. Food Serv. East, Inc., 582 A.2d 1342 (Pa. Super. Ct. 1990).

had told other children of her plans to kill herself. The counselors interviewed Nicole, who denied making such statements, but neither of the counselors notified Nicole's parents or school administrators. Nicole joined with a friend from another school in a suicide pact, which was carried out on a school holiday, away from school grounds. Nicole's father brought suit against the counselors, alleging breach of their duty to intervene to attempt to prevent the suicide. The circuit court granted summary judgment in favor of the counselors, finding an absence of any such duty.

The court of appeals ruled that the summary judgment was in error, distinguishing the facts in this case from previous case law finding that therapists could rarely be held liable for outpatient suicides. The negligence complained of in *Eisel* was not failure to prevent the suicide by exercising control or custody over Nicole, only the failure to communicate to Nicole's parent information possessed by the counselors. Had the parent been warned of the contemplated suicide, he might have been able to intervene. Second, the school stands *in loco parentis* in its relationship with students, and that results in "a special duty to exercise reasonable care to protect a pupil from harm" (pp. 451–452). Finally, Nicole's counselor was specially trained in crisis intervention techniques, suicide warnings, and crisis psychiatric services.

The court went on to analyze that Nicole's suicide was foreseeable, because the counselors had direct knowledge of Nicole's intent to commit suicide. The state of Maryland and Nicole's school have suicide prevention programs aimed at responding to communicated threats of suicide to intervene, including the recommendation in a policy memorandum to "share your knowledge with parents, friends, teachers or other people who might be able to help. Don't worry about breaking a confidence if someone reveals suicidal plans to you. You may have to betray a secret to save a life" (p. 454). The court went on to discuss whether the breach of the counselors' alleged duty to notify the parents was the proximate cause of the suicide, the concept of moral blame, and the scope of the burden on the counselors to have notified the parents, as measured against the risk of death to a child. Once the facts are fully developed in all these areas, the court concluded, *a jury could find that there is indeed a duty imposed on counselors to notify parents* in the event they receive information about such potential harm.

The cases demonstrate that the courts continue to grapple with the issues of confidentiality and the competing duty to warn potential victims of violent patients or clients, even in cases involving psychiatrists. Some state legislatures are trying to address the issue as well. A

1994 amendment to Virginia law specifically states that mental health providers have a duty to take precautions to protect third parties from violent behavior or serious harm communicated to the counselor by the patient or client. The counselor may seek civil commitment, make reasonable attempts to warn the potential victim, notify the appropriate law enforcement authority, *or provide counseling until the provider reasonably believes the threat is gone* (Code of Virginia, §54.1-2400, 1994). The amendment also makes health care providers immune from civil suit for breaching confidentiality in communicating such threats, failing to predict harm in the absence of a threat, or for failing to take precautions other than those specified in the law. Consequently, as the law in this area continues to evolve, it is important to keep informed of judicial and legislative actions that affect your practice area.

In the absence of state laws such as the one in Virginia, counselors still have an ethical duty to disclose information when required to prevent clear and imminent danger to the client or others. The real question is how to know with certainty that disclosure is required while still protecting the counselor from potential liability?

First, the counselor should have discussed with the client at the outset of the relationship the concept and limits of confidentiality, including the duty to disclose information obtained through counseling to protect the client or others from imminent harm. Once information is revealed that leads the counselor to believe the client may harm himself or another, the counselor should obtain past clinical history from other clinicians or treatment facilities. The issue should be discussed openly and fully with the client. It is important to distinguish between mere fantasizing and a real threat of harm, but once that becomes clear, it is important to document the conversation in the client's records. The remaining guidelines are suggested to afford maximum privacy protection for the client:

1. Consult with another professional or your supervisor. Consult with your attorney if you are concerned about your exposure. Be sure you know if the law in your state requires a communicated threat and a specifically identifiable victim.
2. Make referrals where appropriate.
3. Notify any person who may be responsible for the client or call the police.
4. Notify the intended victim.
5. Consider other solutions, including possible voluntary or involuntary commitment.

At each step the counselor must take care to disclose confidential information only to the extent it is necessary to protect the intended victim or the client and be sure to document that decision making in the client's record. The record should show what options were considered, any consultation or supervision, and the rationale for the decision, including ethical or legal standards or precedents that may apply.

AIDS Cases and Confidentiality

Of all the issues involving a duty to warn on the part of a counselor, perhaps the most difficult involves a client who has been diagnosed with a communicable disease, particularly the human immunodeficiency virus (HIV) and acquired immune deficiency syndrome (AIDS). As discussed, counselors may have no legal duty to disclose information about a client's HIV status to third persons, but if you reasonably believe that your client intends to continue having unprotected sex or sharing needles with unsuspecting but reasonably identifiable third parties, you have an ethical obligation to take some steps to curb the behavior and warn the potential victim(s) (*ACA Code of Ethics* B.1.d.).

Once you determine that your client's behavior requires you to act to warn possible victims, how can you limit your exposure to a lawsuit for violating the client's privacy rights? As emphasized earlier, the first step is to review again with your client the limits of confidentiality you (one hopes) discussed with him at the beginning of the counseling relationship. Make sure he recognizes your legal *and* ethical duties. Ahia and Martin (1993) also specified a series of steps counselors should take:

1. Get the latest medical information about AIDS transmission and advise all clients to practice safe sex.
2. Review the HIV confidentiality law of your state.
3. Once you learn a client is HIV positive, provide him or her with clear information on practicing safe sex and encourage the client to inform sex partners and others who may be at risk.
4. Before you disclose the client's HIV status to another person, it is usually advisable to discuss your intention to do so with the client.
5. Limit the information you disclose to a potential victim about your client's HIV status to that which is absolutely necessary to protect the potential victim, being careful to follow statutory guidelines and safeguard the client's privacy as much as possible.

It is important to remember that the mere fact that a client is HIV positive is extremely sensitive. Revealing such information may not strictly violate state AIDS disclosure laws, but, unless the individual gives consent or refuses to tell a partner or other potential victim, there is no privilege for breaching an individual's right to privacy on this issue. Even when the individual is incarcerated, he or she retains the right to privacy. A Wisconsin case is illustrative (*Hillman v. Columbia County*, 1991). In that case Hillman's medical records showing he was hospitalized with AIDS were sent to the county jail where he was incarcerated. Soon after, he discovered that many inmates and jail employees knew of his AIDS status. He sued jail employees and the county for violation of his right to privacy and won on appeal. The employee-defendants were held liable for disclosing Hillman's AIDS status to nonmedical personnel, which was not part of their job responsibilities.

Counseling Minors

Virtually all the standards for protecting client confidences that apply to adults are equally applicable to minors (children under the age of 18). According to Remley (1985), this includes the rights to be informed before information is disclosed to others, to be involved in decision-making, and to be kept informed of decisions as they are made. Certainly some information revealed in counseling sessions would be detrimental to family relationships if divulged to parents or guardians and would destroy the trust between the client and counselor. Yet clearly parents, who are legally and financially responsible for the upbringing of their children, have some right to know what is learned in the counseling process. In addition, counselors may feel that sharing information with particular adults could further the progress of counseling.

The *ACA Code of Ethics* permits involving parents or guardians in the counseling process as appropriate, so long as the counselor acts in the best interest of the client and takes measures to safeguard confidentiality (B.3.). So again, the counselor has a balancing test: Is the client's right to confidentiality outweighed by the need to inform a parent, guardian, or other adult of information received in the course of counseling? Many factors should be considered in the analysis, including the age and educational level of the client; the relationship with parents or guardians; whether disclosure can reasonably be expected to help the situation or could cause harm; and the severity of potential harm or injury that could come if the information is not disclosed (is the client smoking tobacco or using drugs?). Counselors should also take into account whether the minor client has been consulted about the disclosure and the position or relationship of the adult who has requested information.

Requests for information about a minor client from nonparents are frequent in the school setting. Sharing student information with teachers and administrators is common in schools and is usually considered necessary to the progress of the student but should be limited to the "educational need to know" situation. According to Salo and Shumate (1993), counselors should keep in mind that the privacy rights of a student, unlike those of an adult, legally belong to the parent or guardian, and parental permission should be obtained before sensitive confidential information is divulged to a third person.

Counselors in schools that receive federal funding are generally bound by the provisions of the Family Educational Rights and Privacy Act of 1974 (FERPA, or the Buckley Amendment), the implementing regulations (Privacy Rights of Parents and Students), and state and local school board policies concerning the disclosure of educational records of students. Within the context of these controlling provisions, counselors must exercise discretion about the extent of the information to be released to parents from their personal records of confidential counseling sessions. There may be times when a counselor would choose not to reveal certain information, even to parents. Unless compelled by school board policy or a competing duty to warn or protect, counselors are not required by FERPA to make their personal records available or disclose the substance of confidential counseling sessions to parents.

Questions also have arisen, for example, concerning requests for information from noncustodial parents. The policy of FERPA makes it clear that noncustodial parents have the same rights to educational records as custodial parents in the absence of a court order to the contrary. This does not apply to the personal records of counselors or to sensitive information that may have been revealed by the student. In such cases counselors should obtain permission from the custodial parent before revealing information, particularly about sensitive issues such as the child's relationship with the custodial parent. If that permission is not obtained, do not disclose the information without a court order. The only exception would be if the counselor reasonably believes that, under the *Tarasoff* analysis, failure to contact a noncustodial parent could cause harm to the child.

Group and Family Counseling

The legal concept of privileged communication generally does not apply in group and family counseling. Despite the clear indications that such therapy is effective in proper situations, the privilege generally does not extend to confidences revealed where more than two persons are present, unless there is a statutory exception. Consequently, all members of a counseling group should assume that they could be called to testify in court concerning any information revealed to the group in counseling sessions.

There is, however, an ethical consideration for protecting the confidentiality of group participants, and it is the responsibility of the counselor to address this aspect at the outset of the group relationship. Standard B.2.a. of the *ACA Code of Ethics* requires counselors to "clearly define confidentiality and the parameters for the specific group . . . and discuss the difficulties related to confidentiality." They must also clearly communicate to all members of the group that, even though counselors will not reveal client information, they cannot guarantee that group members will not do so. Although this is not required, it is good practice to ask group members to sign an agreement that they will honor and protect the confidences of other members of the group and understand the consequences of violating that agreement. Counselors should also review the confidentiality agreement with group participants periodically.

Counselors working with family groups also must ensure that all members are aware that their communications within the group will not be considered privileged in a court of law, unless there is a statutory protection in the state. But counselors working with families do not always see the entire family system, and information may be revealed by one family member individually in the course of working with the entire family. Should those communications be protected? The *Code of Ethics* admonishes counselors that "information about one family member cannot be disclosed to another member without permission" and requires counselors to "protect the privacy rights of each family member" (B.2.b.). This includes access to written records, as well as to verbal communication (B.4.d.). The best advice is to set the ground rules for the family group as a whole and be sure they understand the limits of your ethical obligations.

Revealing information about the group, family members, or a family system to individuals outside the counseling relationship should be done only after obtaining a release from all affected group or family members, or upon court order.

Counseling Public Offenders

Probably the greatest problem facing counselors in prisons, prerelease centers and other custodial institutions is the persistence of role conflicts between the ethical guidelines stressing confidentiality and the need to share information among agencies involved in the correctional process. Clients may wish to discuss particular problems, such as drug use in prison, but failing to reveal that information could cost a counselor his or her job. Clients also know that counselors are required to report to courts and correctional officials on the progress of their clients, so they might be inclined to present themselves in a more positive light.

Many state statutes now permit access to prison records beyond the correctional institution to local parole boards, probation departments, and even community service boards, for planning and coordinating postrelease mental health services for offenders. Other than those records restricted by federal law, such as those relating to AIDS or HIV status and substance abuse, virtually all records are available and cannot be protected by counselors.

Despite conflicting job requirements and state laws, public offender counselors still are bound by the ethical duty to maintain their clients' confidences that forms the basis of the counseling relationship. Client confidences must be protected when possible, but clients should be advised at the outset that the information must be included in periodic court reports. They must also understand that criminal activities, including threats of violence, disclosed in counseling must be reported. Counselors should take extra care in maintaining and documenting prison counseling records, and information included in periodic reports should be limited to that which is requested.

Reports and Records

Although clinical records may not be legally mandated in most cases unless required by an employing agency (Remley, 1990), the obligation to provide quality client care probably requires counselors to keep regular, specific clinical notes. Failing to do so could be considered malpractice. In fact, the *ACA Code of Ethics* now requires counselors to "maintain records necessary for rendering professional services to their clients and as required by laws, regulations, or agency or institution procedures" (B.4.a.). Counselors should understand there are ethical and legal reasons to maintain accurate counseling records and a corresponding duty to keep such records confidential. However, circumstances may arise when these records may be required to be disclosed to clients or third parties, so it is imperative that all client records be kept accurately and professionally, and required business and financial records should be maintained separately from any clinical notes that may be taken. This applies to information contained in computer or other electronic data storage systems, as well as written records in paper or microfilm storage files. The section on Records and Record Keeping in Chapter 6 discusses more fully ways of protecting and preserving counseling records.

There are three particular situations in which counselors are required to disclose their records. The first was discussed previously, when the counselor has a duty to protect an intended victim from a client's violent propensities or where the counselor believes the client is a danger to herself. Records might be provided to another mental health professional, a supervisor, or an attorney representing the client for use in commitment proceedings.

The second is where the client requests that records be disclosed to some third party, or to her- or himself. Although the counselor creates the records, clients ordinarily have the right to inspect and obtain copies of the records a professional keeps about them and to request that copies be sent to other mental health professionals, insurance companies, or others. As discussed, however, counselors must exercise care not to release information to third parties without the consent, preferably in writing, of the client.

Finally, counselors must make their records available when required by court order, even if they believe this will violate their professional ethical responsibility to ensure the confidentiality of the counseling relationship. Certainly counselors may protest such orders and advise their clients to do so as well, but they risk facing contempt of court proceedings if they refuse to comply with a court order.

Counselors who work in schools, colleges, or universities that receive federal funding are bound by the record-keeping guidelines of FERPA, which gives students and their parents the right to review all official records, files, and data related to their children and provides that such records may not be released to third parties without the written permission of the student or parents. For purposes of FERPA, educational records generally include all records kept by any employee of an educational institution. However, records made by and kept in the sole possession of a "physician, psychiatrist, psychologist or other recognized professional or paraprofessional acting in his professional or paraprofessional capacity" are excluded from the disclosure requirements, except that notes may be provided to other treating professionals or reviewed by a physician of the student's choice (34 C.F.R. §99.3). Maintaining counseling records in a locked cabinet, accessible only to the counselor, should meet this requirement.

Subpoenas

A subpoena is an official court document that requires the recipient to appear in court to be questioned, or to be deposed at another location, about a lawsuit. Subpoenas may come from attorneys representing your client or someone who is proceeding against your client, and you must respond carefully, unless the subpoena is withdrawn or overruled by a judge. As counselors respond, however, the confidences of clients and any privileged communications must be protected. Subpoenas are generally drafted broadly to elicit as much information as possible, even though that information may not be relevant or may be protected by a privileged communication statute. Consequently, it is important again to understand your state statute concerning privileged communications, who is entitled to authorize you to surrender client information (attorney, judge, client?), and whether it applies to your practice, and to plan in advance the scope of information you are required to reveal in complying with a subpoena.

Bertram and Wheeler (1994) recommend that, if you receive a subpoena, do not automatically respond with the requested information. You should also make sure your employees know how to handle such matters. Consult your attorney or your client's attorney and request guidance. If it is determined you should respond to the subpoena, ask all clients involved in the counseling to sign an Informed Consent to Release Information that indicates what information will be released and to whom. Further, if your client's attorney does not want the information released, ask that a motion to quash the subpoena be filed that, if granted, will protect you from responding to the subpoena. Be sure to keep copies of all documents and notes in the client's record about all conversations with your client and his attorney about the subpoena.

Court Appearances

Counselors may be called to testify in court in a variety of capacities arising from their professional counseling experience. First is the situation where a counselor is paid to render services as an expert witness to help judges and juries reach their decision. A monograph in the ACA Legal Series is devoted to counselors as expert witnesses (Weikel & Hughes, 1993) and is well worth consulting prior to embarking on this type of service to the court and community. Expert witnesses are usually hired by one side in a dispute or appointed by the court and may provide testimony based solely on knowledge and expertise. Alternatively, a counselor may be asked to evaluate a party and form opinions to be divulged in court. In either case, the ethical confidentiality rules probably are not applicable.

The most common circumstance where counselors are likely to encounter the conflict between ethical privacy considerations and court-ordered requests for information is when the counselor is called as a witness of fact to testify as to information collected during counseling sessions with a client or when the counselor is a defendant herself. Obviously the ethical duty to protect a client's privacy rights does not terminate when the counselor enters the courtroom, but unless the counselor-client interaction is protected by a privileged communication statute in your state, you may be ordered to reveal private information. Counselors are urged to explain to the judge in the proceeding that they are ethically obligated to safeguard the confidences of their clients and to request that they not be required to reveal confidential client information. If the judge orders the testimony nonetheless, then counselors must comply. Questions posed in court should be answered truthfully, but counselors should not volunteer additional information concerning the client. Counselors appearing in court to testify usually will be under the direction of an attorney and should plan to consult with the attorney in advance about the planned testimony and any concerns about confidentiality.

Despite utmost attention to the legal and ethical aspects of professional practice, counselors occasionally are accused of wrongdoing by a client and are called to appear before state administrative agencies, professional credentialing and disciplinary boards, or courts of law. If you are named as a defendant in a lawsuit, be sure to notify your insurance carrier without delay and call your attorney if one is not appointed for you by the insurance company. Do not attempt to represent yourself or try to reason with your former client, and do not discuss the case with anyone without your attorney's consent. Above all, do not admit negligence or fault to anyone. Finally, remember that you are still obligated to protect your former client's privacy, so do not reveal client information to anyone except your attorney.

Recommendations for Practice

A counselor's duty to maintain client confidences is clearly central to the development of an effective counseling relationship. Yet counselors may find that that duty directly conflicts with their obligations to report abuse or criminal activity, to reveal client information when requested by insurance companies, court subpoenas, educational institutions, or investigative agencies, or to warn potential victims of a client's violent intentions. This chapter has illustrated some of the many situations in which counselors must balance competing duties. It is critical that counselors make decisions based on complete, timely information about ethical standards and state statutes on a case-by-case basis. In this rapidly changing area of the law, counselors can protect themselves from liability in several ways.

First, counselors should know and follow the *ACA Code of Ethics* to the extent those standards apply. Although they do not cover all potential situations, the standards are the best source of information on acceptable conduct for counselors. The advice of other professional counselors may also be instrumental in avoiding possible pitfalls. Many agencies and institutions also have in-house attorneys to advise staff on matters that arise in the course of employment. They should be consulted, where available, for advice concerning specific situations. Counselors who are insured by the ACA Insurance Trust may also call the Risk Management Hotline for risk management guidance.

Second, counselors should keep records and reports current and accurate and carefully preserve any authorizations from clients for release of information. Clients should be made to understand the concept of confidentiality, its limits under your state law, and your other professional responsibilities as well. This should occur at the outset of the counseling relationship, and clients should be reminded of your discussions from time to time. It is also important to ensure that the staff of the counseling office, including secretaries and student interns, fully understand the concept of confidentiality and abide by its dictates. Clear policies should be developed and followed for the retention and eventual destruction of client records.

Third, counselors should discuss cases only with necessary professionals and other parties in a manner that preserves the confidential nature of the information. Counselors should take care that such conversations are not overheard by other people not directly involved in the care or treatment of the client. If there is doubt as to whether certain information should be disclosed, the matter should be discussed with a supervisor or independent legal counsel before the information is disclosed.

Finally, counselors should consider liability insurance coverage. Although such coverage cannot prevent a lawsuit and possible liability, it can provide for the payment of legal fees and costs, as well as for damages, in the event there is a judgment against the counselor.

CHAPTER 5

AVOIDING LIABILITY

C hapter 3 focused on the professional relationships between counselors and their clients and the fiduciary and contractual duties that arise from those relationships. One of those duties, subject to a variety of limitations, is to protect client confidences in order to further the relationship, as discussed in Chapter 4. Counselors also are obligated in a variety of other areas by their professional practice and must take steps to comply with those duties whenever possible.

Competence and Preparation

Perhaps the fundamental goal of professional preparation and competence is to protect clients from harm, much as the fundamental goal of law is to protect society. Just what level of professional preparation and competence is required of a counselor obviously varies depending on the area of counseling in which he or she practices. Four general areas of professional competence were outlined by Robinson and Gross (1986). These include: (1) professional growth through continuing education; (2) maintaining accurate knowledge and expertise in specialized areas; (3) accurately representing professional qualifications; and (4) providing only services for which one is qualified. These areas may be investigated by state and professional regulatory boards for varying counseling areas and are supported by the *ACA Code of Ethics*.

For example, the *ACA Code of Ethics* specifies that

> Counselors practice only within the boundaries of their competence, based on their education, training, supervised experience, state and

national professional credentials, and appropriate professional experience. Counselors will demonstrate a commitment to gain knowledge, personal awareness, sensitivity, and skills pertinent to working with a diverse client population (C.2.a.).

Counselors are also admonished to complete appropriate training and supervised experience before entering into practice in a new specialty area, to ensure their own competence, and to protect others in the process (C.2.b.). They are also required to accept employment only in positions for which they are qualified and to hire only counselors who are qualified and competent (C.2.c.). As Robinson (1988) explained, "it is not enough to read about or to attend a seminar on new techniques or approaches or special client problems. Only through specific training (advanced educational course work) and experience (under close supervision) are new skills and areas of expertise developed" (p. 4).

Similarly, counselors may claim or imply only those professional credentials they actually possess and are responsible for correcting any known misrepresentations of their credentials by others (C.4.a.). Thus if a client calls a counselor "doctor" and the counselor does not possess that degree, the counselor is ethically obliged to bring the error to the client's attention immediately. Several state licensing, certification, and registration statutes recognize specific credentials for counselors. Since 1992 the American Counseling Association has recognized counselors who have met certain minimum qualifications by the designation "professional counselor." Only counselors who have earned these distinctions by successfully completing the requisite master's level or higher accredited counseling programs may refer to themselves as professional counselors. The appropriate use of this designation is important to the identity of the counseling profession as viewed by the public. As Remley (1993) pointed out, however, "If you are in a state that regulates the title and practice of professional counseling, use the term only if you are registered, certified or licensed."

It is crucial that all counselors follow these ethical standards and consciously strive to work within the limits of their own professional training. Although this seems to be an ethical position, it is also important from a legal standpoint as part of the analysis of a claim of negligence or malpractice, because a counselor's legal duty to a client is largely determined by professional identity.[1] How the counselor holds

---

[1]For example, in Taylor v. Georgia, 404 S.E.2d 255 (Ga. Sup. Ct. 1991), a psychologist with a doctorate in counseling, not psychology, was competent to

himself or herself out to the public will determine the expected practice standards by which he or she may be judged. Counselors who hold themselves out or advertise themselves as specializing in a given area will be judged according to the extraordinary level of skill required of a specialist. As you might guess, this could have disastrous results if the counselor intended only to advertise that his practice is limited to particular areas.

One last area to note in discussing competence is that counselors must not provide "professional services when their physical, mental, or emotional problems are likely to harm a client or others" (C.2.g.). It is also important to recognize the signs of impairment, whether the problem is mental or physical health, substance abuse, or prescription medication reactions, and seek help in a timely manner. It also may be necessary to limit, suspend, or terminate professional responsibilities altogether during periods of impairment, and this is contemplated by the *ACA Code of Ethics* as well (C.2.g.).

Duty of Care and Potential Liability

Professional counselors must exercise *due care* in their counseling relationships or face potential liability in a civil suit for failing to perform their duties as required by law. Civil liability, stated simply, means that one can be sued in a court of law for acting wrongly toward another or for failing to act when there was a recognized duty to do so, that results in injury to another. Judicial relief is usually in the form of money damages awarded to the injured party to compensate for the injuries inflicted.

For counselors, the primary area in which civil liability is found rests in the law of torts. A *tort* is basically a private injury against the person, property, or reputation of another individual that legal action is designed to set right. Torts can take various forms and fall into two categories. The first is the *unintentional* violation of an obligation one person owes to another, such as a counselor's obligation to use all of his or her care and skill in dealing with a client, but it may also include failing to follow all the requirements of a protective statute. This is called *negligence*.

---

testify in court as an expert in forensic psychology. The psychologist had a bachelor's degree in psychology, at least one third of his master's degree coursework was in psychology, and his doctorate courses were equally divided between counseling and psychology.

There are four elements to be proven in a negligence action. First, there must be a *legal duty* arising from a "special relationship" between the parties that will be determined by the facts of the situation. Whether casual conversation at a cocktail party or giving an informational lecture at a local civic gathering constitutes the existence of a special relationship is questionable, but counselors should be circumspect about giving such advice without adequate disclaimers. A court will then look to the professional identity of the counselor to determine what skills and experience he or she should be expected to have and by what standards of practice he or she should be bound. In many cases this will be determined by state licensing, certification, or registration statutes.

Second, the legal duty arising from that relationship must have been *breached*. That is, the mental health professional failed to uphold the standard of care or practice expected of a counselor in that position or violated some law, such as failing to report suspected child abuse or neglect.

Third, there must have been an *actual injury* to the plaintiff, such as emotional distress, loss of self-esteem, or depression, that is evidenced by specific symptoms, worsening of problems, changes in life circumstances, or the like. Generally, some evidence of financial loss also is presented.

Finally, the plaintiff must prove *causation*. That is, the injuries received would not have occurred but for the counselor's breach of duty. Even though there may have been other contributing causes, if the injury to the client was foreseeable and resulted from the counselor's conduct, the counselor can be held liable for damages.

This is a very simplified explanation of a complicated analysis that captivates lawyers and law students, but it should raise a variety of questions about the entire picture of professional practice for mental health practitioners, therapists, and counselors.

The second category of tort occurs where there has been a direct, *intentional*, abrogation of some person's legal rights, such as the invasion of privacy through an illegal search. Other intentional torts include defamation of character, assault, battery, infliction of emotional distress, or any intentional violation of a protected interest.

A counselor might be held liable for one of the intentional torts, *even though the conduct was unintentional*, if the resulting injury was substantially certain to occur from the counselor's act. This might be more likely in counseling relationships than elsewhere because of the intimate nature of counseling. Counselors should be more aware of the particular vulnerabilities of their clients and may be judged on that basis.

An injured person frequently will allege two or more separate causes of action at the same time, for example, claiming that an alleged inappropriate touching was an assault that caused emotional distress. The same alleged injury could also form the basis for a claimed breach of fiduciary and contractual duty.

Certainly few counselors ever anticipate that they might become defendants in a criminal action simply by practicing their profession. But counselors should be aware of certain occupational hazards that could lead to criminal liability. The ideal for professional counselors is to maintain a certain distance between themselves and their clients so they may advise clients in a professional, or clinical, manner. Occasionally, however, situations arise that might lead counselors to go much further in protecting their clients or providing emotional support and comfort than the law literally allows. In such cases a counselor may unwittingly risk criminal liability as an accessory to a crime, for failure to report child abuse, contributing to the delinquency of a minor, insurance fraud, or, most common, sexual misconduct.

In addition to the possibility of administrative sanctions and civil or criminal liability, the costs of defending even a baseless allegation can be significant. No professionals can totally insulate themselves from frivolous claims, but exposure can be limited by careful attention to the duties arising from the counseling relationship. Counselors must have a clear understanding of their professional identity, the nature of the professional relationship, the level of professional preparation and competence necessary, the duty of care expected of a counseling professional, and the standards of practice or code of ethics that establish the permissible boundaries of conduct for the profession and their area of practice.

Malpractice

Malpractice is the term that primarily concerns most professional counselors. As applied to counselors, the term means a lawsuit based on negligence in carrying out professional responsibilities or duties. It is important to recognize that professional malpractice is regulated by state law and usually applies only where the professional person is licensed, certified, or otherwise registered according to state statute. However, other counseling professionals can still be held liable for their actions based on a negligence theory, intentional infliction of emotional distress, or other torts even if malpractice does not technically apply.

Malpractice is usually found in a limited variety of situations including: (1) the procedure followed by the counselor was not within the realm of accepted professional practice; (2) the technique used was one the counselor was not trained to use (lack of professional competence); (3) the counselor failed to follow a procedure that would have been more helpful; (4) the counselor failed to warn others about and protect them from a violent client; (5) informed consent to treatment was not obtained; and (6) the counselor failed to explain the possible consequences of the treatment.

Just as in the analysis for negligence, to establish a case of professional malpractice, the following must all exist:

1. A duty must be owed the plaintiff by the defendant.
2. That duty must have been breached.
3. The plaintiff must have been injured.
4. The injury sustained was caused by the defendant's breach of duty.

The "duty" owed by the counselor is premised on the existence of a *fiduciary relationship* between the counselor and the client, as discussed in Chapter 3, one that fosters the highest level of trust and confidence. The client has the right to expect the highest level of care from the counselor, and the counselor is obligated to provide that standard of care.

The primary problem in a malpractice suit is to determine which standard of care to apply to ascertain whether a counselor has breached his duty to a client. Professional malpractice is generally judged by whether a reasonably prudent *counselor* in the same or similar circumstance would have acted in the same manner as the counselor did. If the answer is "yes," liability usually will not be found. However, when the counselor holds herself out as an expert in a particular discipline, she must then meet the standard of care required of an expert in that area. Psychiatrists will be held to a higher standard of care, for example, than counselors with master's degrees. The courts also look to licensing, certification, or registration statutes, as well as professional standards of practice and codes of ethics, to determine the standard of care to apply in each situation. Courts also borrow from case precedents set in other related professions such as psychiatry, psychology, medicine, and law to measure counselor performance.

Malpractice claims may arise from a variety of issues in the counseling relationship, although all share the common elements of professional duty of care, breach of that duty, resulting injury, and causation. Watch for these elements in the examples that follow.

Diagnosis and Scope of Treatment

The education, training, experience, and other qualifications required for a mental health counselor to render specific mental health diagnoses are set out in state licensing laws. Thus counselors have the duty to render mental health diagnoses that they are competent to render and with the care and skill expected of other counselors who hold similar qualifying licenses. Obviously, giving a diagnosis you are not qualified or licensed to render could leave you vulnerable to subsequent liability for malpractice.

In addition to the statutory duty to determine a diagnosis and course of treatment, licensed counselors have the ethical obligation to "take special care to provide a proper diagnosis of mental disorders. Assessment techniques (including personal interview) used to determine client care (e.g., locus of treatment, type of treatment, or recommended follow-up) are carefully selected and appropriately used" (E.5.a.). Failure to use appropriate assessment tools, including testing irregularities, could result in an improper diagnosis and could also constitute a breach of the counselor's duty of care.

Your determination that a client has a condition requiring medical psychotherapeutic treatment generally also will define the appropriate treatment regimen that is considered the standard of care for that diagnosis. The treatment you provide the client must be consistent with the accepted standard of care for that treatment to avoid potential liability.

Failure to Treat or Refer

The counselor's primary ethical responsibility is to respect the dignity and promote the welfare of clients. Coupled with the legal duty to render competent diagnoses and provide proper treatment based on training, skill, and experience, these establish the standard of practice the counselor is expected to meet with each client. This may sound fairly simple, but in day-to-day practice myriad complications arise that complicate the counseling relationship and the responsibilities of the counselor.

Generally speaking, courts will not find counselors negligent merely because the client fails to improve during the counseling relationship or if the approach the counselor chooses in treatment proves to be erroneous. Courts have ruled that no presumption of negligence arises from a mere mistake in judgment if that mistake is the type that could be made by the most careful and skilled practitioner of the counseling art. Again, however, the counselor will be judged according to standards applicable to the counseling profession.[2]

Counselors are reminded that the initial disclosure meeting with clients should include a discussion of the limits of the proposed course of treatment, as well as the potential risks and benefits. Only under extremely rare circumstances could a counselor be held liable for promising improvement so long as he or she pursues a course of treatment dictated by licensing standards and the ethics and standards of the profession. This has been recognized in cases dealing with psychiatric treatment (see *Johnston v. Rodis*, 1958), and there is every reason to believe this rule would apply to a counselor, who, in the absence of some ill motive, advises a particular course of action that is later found not to have worked.

A more difficult situation arises when a counselor determines, or should have determined, that a course of therapy or treatment is not effective for the client, or if the problems presented are beyond the competence of the counselor. In those cases there is a clear professional ethical duty to seek consultation with another competent professional or to terminate the counseling relationship and refer the client to another qualified professional (A.11.b and A.11.c). There may also be a legal duty to consult or refer when the counselor is not competent to meet the client's needs, but at this point it seems a client could sustain a claim for malpractice only if he can show that improvement, of which there was a substantial likelihood, was prevented because the counselor breached the duty to refer the client or consult with another professional concerning treatment. This would be extremely difficult to prove in a counseling relationship, but liability was found in at least one case involving a physician who failed to refer a patient with Graves disease to a specialist (*Wozniak v. Lifoff*, 1988).[3]

Two decisions reflect the confusion in this area about when a counselor should determine that referral or consultation is necessary. The

---

[2]In Grote v. J.S. Mayer & Co., Inc., 570 N.E.2d 1146 (Ohio Ct. App. 1990), a case about failure to refer, the court determined that the claim could not be proved without using expert testimony to guide the jury on the standard of care required. Presumably, this would require the testimony of a similarly licensed professional.

[3]In this case the physician was an inexperienced internist who not only failed to refer the patient but also prescribed medication that the patient eventually used to kill herself.

first involves an industrial psychologist who administered a series of vocational skills tests to a client in 1975 and met with him four more times in the next year. There was only limited telephone contact with the client after that time, most recently in the fall of 1982. In 1990 the psychologist was called to court to defend claims that he had failed to refer the client to a clinical psychologist for treatment of his mental illness, prevented him from seeking appropriate treatment, and aggravated his condition. As it turned out, the court dismissed the client's claim because he did not bring an expert to testify about the psychologist's breach of duty, but depending on the circumstances not found in the case report, it is possible that a referral should have been made during the initial testing and evaluation (*Grote v. J.S. Mayer & Co., Inc.,* 1990).

The other area involves members of the clergy. *Nally v. Grace Community Church* (1984, 1987, 1988, 1989), involved a young man who committed suicide after counseling by a minister in California. Among the issues was whether the client should have been referred to someone more competent to handle his problems. The California Supreme Court refused to hold the pastoral counselor liable for failing either to refer the young man to another professional or to warn the client's parents that their son was on the verge of suicide.

Group Counseling

Group therapy has developed into a widely accepted means of treatment for a variety of counseling needs. It is believed the clients learn to understand and communicate more effectively with peers and that they are better able to put their anxieties or fears into perspective than could be achieved through individual counseling. Counselors leading groups must be well trained and skillful in their use of this technique and must be careful to follow accepted standards of practice with groups. As discussed, the concept of privileged communication does not generally apply in group settings except where it is expressly granted by state statute. Consequently, the counselor must inform all group participants of the limits of confidentiality within the group setting, their responsibilities to other group members, and the absence of the legal privilege concerning group discussions.

But the counselor's duty to each member of a group is the same as in individual counseling sessions: Professional services must be rendered according to the recognized standard of care expected of a competent counselor. Should the counselor fail to bring to that relationship the skill and care of a qualified counselor practicing within the expert discipline of the profession, the counselor may be liable for breach of professional duty to clients. However, the legal requirement of care is more complicated in the group relationship than in the individual counseling setting, for several reasons. First, the counselor may be responsible for forming the group and selecting the members. Once the group is formed, the counselor bears the increased duty of supervising the multiple interactions among the various group members and for protecting each member of the group from physical and/or psychological trauma that may result from the group setting.

Counselors must constantly evaluate the size of the group, its appropriateness for each particular member, whether to refer individual members of the group for special help, and whether to bring in an additional counseling professional to assist in the group sessions. Counselors must also be alert to unanticipated encounters within a group and be prepared to handle potentially explosive situations with a high degree of professional skill to protect each individual member of the group. This requires extensive training and preparation to avoid potential liability.

The *Ethical Guidelines for Group Counselors* (Association for Specialists in Group Work, 1989) provide an excellent discussion of the responsibilities of the counselor in group work, in terms of providing both adequate information to clients and group counseling services. The guidelines stress the need to prepare clients adequately before they enter the group so that they are fully informed, screening members before they are admitted to a group, setting a norm of confidentiality among group members, protecting group clients from undue pressure or coercion, treating each member of a group individually and equally, and ensuring proper follow-up for group members who choose to leave the group prematurely. The guidelines also emphasize the need for adequate professional preparation before practicing group therapy, as well as ongoing assessment of the group experience. Because a court may take such professional standards into account when judging whether the actions of a group counselor have been negligent, counselors should become familiar with these guidelines and make every effort to provide services accordingly.

One additional note of caution should be sounded. As in all counseling situations, the group counselor has the obligation to remain objective and use good professional judgment with all group members. From time to time, it may be difficult to abide by this dictate with some group members. Consider the situation where one experienced group leader found himself so angry with one group member's repeated personal and physical attacks that he felt compelled to return the attack physically. Recognizing that these feelings violated his professional responsibility both to the group and to the disruptive client, the counselor immediately sought the help of a professional colleague to deal with his own anger and frustration. A less experienced counselor may not have acted so responsibly, and a malpractice action could have resulted.

Crisis Intervention

Crisis intervention, or crisis management, as a counseling technique is unique and, of course, generally arises out of an emergency situation. The person who needs assistance may be only a short step from death or serious injury, and the counselor serves merely as a buffer, hoping to avert tragedy or hold off self-destructive acts or impulses until appropriate medical or mental health treatment can be provided.

In a crisis intervention situation the counselor generally has no real control over the person who seeks help. The counselor serves as a rescuer, attempting to ward off disaster until help arrives. The general legal principle that applies to rescuers is this: *A person is responsible for harm to another only if the failure to exercise reasonable care increases the risk of harm to another.* The counselor offers to listen to the distressed person, provides words of encouragement or suggestions, and has a duty to use his or her training and skill to assist the distressed individual until therapy or medical treatment can be provided. This does not mean that the counselor is responsible for knowing the history or problems of the person being counseled that are not revealed during the crisis intervention. Consequently the counselor will be subject to a negligence suit *only* if the counselor fails to use reasonable care in counseling *and* that failure increases the risk of harm to the person. Even if the counselor did not use reasonable care, the counselor will not be held liable for negligence unless that failure *also* increased the risk of harm or left the person in a worse position than before.

It should be noted that the term *client* has not been used to describe the person being counseled in crisis intervention because that denotes the existence of a relationship between the crisis intervention counselor and the individual in need of assistance. If such a relationship exists, however, the counselor may be held to the same standard of care described previously for the counselor-client relationship. So, for example, consider the counselor who works on a crisis intervention hotline one night each week. One evening he takes a call from someone by whose voice and difficulties he recognizes as a client. In that situation the counselor may have a greater duty to warn family members or provide immediate assistance because the preexisting professional relationship would be presumed to have provided the counselor with sufficient knowledge to render real assistance.

Repressed or False Memory

If the increased number of queries from counselors is any indication, the validity of past memories of child sexual abuse is the new "hot topic" in the mental health professions. The level of concern is certainly valid, considering that a jury in Ramsey County, Minnesota, reportedly awarded more than $2.6 million to a woman who claimed she was injured by false memories of abuse induced after her psychiatrist told her she suffered from multiple personality disorder, probably as the result of repeated sexual abuse by relatives (Woman in False-Memory Case, 1995).

Debate over repressed, and possibly false, memory has also been lively within the American Psychiatric Association (APA), which released a "Fact Sheet" on the topic in April 1994. The material and recommendations that follow are largely drawn from that report.

Concerns in this area stem from the increased numbers of reports of cases of child sexual abuse that cannot be documented or otherwise corroborated, as well as the increased number of cases that can be verified and the techniques used to reveal these memories. What is known is that child sexual abuse is a risk factor in a variety of psychiatric disorders. Children who have been abused may try to cope with the trauma in a variety of ways, some of which may cause a lack of conscious awareness of the abuse for some time. The memories and feelings resulting from the abuse may emerge at a later time. Questioning can influence memories, particularly in young children, and repeated questioning can lead an individual to believe in a "memory" of an event that did not occur. Finally, even without an initial recollection of abuse, a trusted person who suggests that as a possible explanation for problems or symptoms can have significant influence.

How should a counselor respond when signs of past sexual abuse are revealed in counseling to protect the client, the alleged abuser, and other family members, without exposing herself to potential liability? First and foremost, follow the basic clinical and ethical principles:

- Be attentive to the kinds of questions you ask.
- Remain empathetic and nonjudgmental in your responses and in conversations with the client about possible memories of abuse.
- Avoid prejudging the truth of the client's reports.

- If a client raises the issue, talk frankly about the clinical uncertainty of such memories at this time.
- Follow established assessment and treatment techniques.
- Be cautious not to pressure the client to believe events that may not have occurred.
- Caution the client not to break off relationships precipitously.
- If you are not specifically trained and competent in this area, consult with a supervisor or more qualified colleague, or refer the client, to avoid providing inadequate care.

Remember also not to accept blindly the judgment of another therapist on treatment in this area. Keep in mind that you may have a duty under state law to report the alleged child sexual abuse at some point once you are convinced of the likelihood it actually occurred. Finally, be sure to carefully document the client's files as to the alleged facts, the circumstances under which the repressed memory was revealed, the techniques you employed to evaluate and assess the veracity of the memory, and the various treatment options you have considered, including consultation or referral to other colleagues.

Hopkins (1995) points out the difficulties counselors face in dealing with issues of repressed memories given the uncertainty, media attention, and destructive potential, and sets out basic guiding principles that are consistent with the approach taken by the APA. Her recommendation for counselors in such troubling circumstances is that "re-establishing the time-honored and proven skills we learned in the counseling lab will get us back onto firm ground. Sometimes our solutions lie not in more and more complicated techniques and theories, but in the simple basic principles of the helping relationship."

Responsibility for Supervision

Supervisors and consultants are an important resource for handling issues that may arise with a counseling client in an effort to make reasonable standard-of-care decisions. Such consultation may help to avoid issues that could give rise to potential liability and provide some corroborating testimony if it becomes necessary, but legal exposure can also result from the consultative or supervisory relationship itself. This is true whether the nature of the supervisory relationship is determined by two colleagues who agree to be available for consultation on occasion as needed or whether the relationship is framed as direct supervision in a clinical setting where an inexperienced counselor is working to gain the requisite skills and experience. In both cases supervision is a formal process whereby a standard of care is being communicated to the counselor being supervised, and the supervising counselor has an obligation to ensure that the supervisee is providing that standard of care to his or her clients.

In the context of clinical supervision a supervisor may be held legally liable for injuries to clients caused by the negligence of a supervisee if those acts occurred in the course and scope of the supervisory relationship. Courts will look to a number of factors to determine whether the supervisor should be held accountable, including the supervisor's control over the supervisee, the location and time at which the act occurred, whether the negligent act was within the supervisee's scope of duty, the supervisee's motivation, and whether the negligent act may have been foreseeable. According to Disney and Stephens (1994), if a court determines that the injury occurred within the course and scope of the supervisory relationship, "then the supervisor is held vicariously liable for the harm caused by the negligence of the supervisee" (p. 17).

Most would agree that the process of supervision is critical to the profession's ability to deliver counseling services that meet acceptable standard of care. Yet supervising counselors need to minimize their exposure to liability as they perform this service to the profession as much as possible. Recognizing that supervisors can be drawn into malpractice cases because of the acts of their supervisees is the first step. Prudence dictates that supervisors and supervisees take other steps to protect themselves and their clients as well. First, establish the ground rules of the relationship. Crawford (1994) cautions that both supervisor and supervisee agree on

> the nature of the assistance to be given and received. Is it supervision (both direct and vicarious responsibility of the supervisor for the counselor's services to the client), consultation (responsibility of the consultant only to the counselor), informal advice giving (no responsibility to anyone, although the advice is seriously given), or mere casual conversation (p. 70).

Be sure both parties agree on the nature of this relationship and the legal implications. Discuss the possibility of testifying and sharing liability at the outset. Plan sufficient time for contact and communication to permit complete discussion of cases and document those supervisory sessions, no matter how informal they may seem. Agree on procedures for preserving records and evidence of decision making. Finally, supervising counselors must ensure that their supervisees are competent and should assess the relationship periodically to ensure that proper procedures are being followed.

One last note on supervising participants in a peer counseling program, where students are specially trained to offer support and guidance in specific, limited areas to their peers. Just as in other direct supervisory programs, a supervising counselor may be held responsible for the acts of peer counselors. Be certain that all students understand the limits and scope of the program they are working within, including issues relating to confidentiality. If situations arise that are beyond the level of their expertise, be sure they know to report back to the supervisor immediately.

Birth Control and Abortion Counseling

Most counselors who work with minors will be confronted with requests for information and advice concerning birth control and abortions at some point in their careers. Counselors employed by state welfare and family planning agencies certainly deal with such requests on a daily basis. In fact, many state welfare systems include funds for dissemination of family planning information to their clients. In addition to the obvious public acceptance of the practice of birth control, sex and family life education classes are now mandated in many state school systems. Many local jurisdictions have established adolescent health clinics that are empowered to dispense birth control and family planning information to minors who seek their services. Furthermore, in the aftermath of the AIDS epidemic, public service announcements on radio, television, and in print media openly discuss the use of condoms and advocate "safe sex." Minor children are confronted with these messages on a daily basis.

Unfortunately, despite the widespread availability of this information, many fail to take advantage of the services or use the information effectively. The resulting pregnancies take their toll on health, education, and social services and particularly on the emotional and psychological well-being of the teenagers who become pregnant. It is apparent that counselors will continue to field queries concerning contraception and family planning in the foreseeable future, so it is important to understand the appropriate boundaries of assistance that may be given.

Counselors are generally free to inform clients of the availability of birth control methods without fear of legal liability and to refer clients to family planning or health clinics for more information. In a few states, however, counselors might be held accountable for providing such information to minors without the consent of their parents. Birth control for adolescents remains a highly emotional issue in many communities, and parental consent may be the preferred avenue in some jurisdictions. Referral to a health clinic or physician is always appropriate when minors request contraceptive information or advice. If the counselor decides to provide birth control information, it must be both accurate and complete, and it is important that the client fully understand the information given. Some school boards prescribe that information concerning abstinence also be provided, so it is important that counselors be informed of local rules and statutes in this area.

Advising clients, whether minors or adults, concerning birth control is to be distinguished from counseling such clients about abortions, particularly when the client is already pregnant. Counselors must be cautious not to impose their own views on clients in this highly emotional area and may in fact be restricted from even mentioning the concept of abortion if they work in a federally funded family practice clinic. Thus it is critical that counselors be aware of the limits of information that may be provided and exercise great care to provide information that is accurate.

Since 1973 abortions have been legal in the United States, subject to a trimester test, based upon a woman's constitutionally protected right to privacy as set out in *Roe v. Wade* (1973). Subsequent statutes and court decisions have limited that right in some states for minors, who must obtain parental consent or a court order prior to the abortion saying that the abortion is in her best interest. Public funding of abortions may be restricted in some states as well, following the Supreme Court's decision in *Webster v. Reproductive Health Services* (1989). *Webster* upheld the Missouri statute that also requires physicians to test for fetal viability at 20 weeks, two thirds of the way through the second trimester of a pregnancy, a test that may eventually come to surpass the straight trimester test of *Roe v. Wade,* which presently restricts abortions during the third trimester, except where the life or health of the mother is in jeopardy. Many states also require informed consent, parental consent in the case of minors, and spousal notification, except in limited situations.

Three particular concepts are important to counselors. First, the right to an abortion is guaranteed by the U.S. Constitution. States may regulate the performance of abortions, however, to protect the health and safety of their citizens. Furthermore, states are not obligated to provide public funding for abortions and may be restricted from providing information about abortion as an option in counseling a client (*Rust v. Sullivan*, 1991).[4]

---

[4]Rust v. Sullivan upheld a federal regulation forbidding clinics that receive federal funds from counseling women about the availability of abortion, even if

Second, the Court has ruled that parents of an unmarried pregnant minor have some rights to know about and consent to an abortion. But there must be some means by which a minor can prove her maturity, demonstrate informed consent to the procedure, and, despite parental objection, obtain a court order permitting an abortion.

Finally, physicians are the proper persons to advise pregnant women on the abortion procedure and assist in their decision making. Such duties can be delegated to other individuals either supervised by the physician or specially trained to provide all the information needed. If you do not have the special training contemplated by laws in your state, a knowledgeable referral is the prudent course.

Sexual Misconduct

Section A.7.a. of the *ACA Code of Ethics* specifically forbids any type of sexual relations with current clients and requires counselors not to counsel anyone with whom they have had a sexual relationship. Further, the ethical code restricts counselors from becoming involved sexually with a *former* client within a minimum of 2 years following termination of counseling. Even after that time, the counselor still has the obligation to put the best interests of the client first and must ensure that the relationship is not exploitative. Virtually every professional code of ethics for practitioners of healing arts contains language prohibiting sexual relationships with clients, and for good reason. The violation of boundaries and professional trust is damaging to the client and the counseling relationship, violates the standard of care expected of professional counselors, and exposes the counselor to criminal liability in many states. Despite public condemnation by all the major mental health organizations and considerable publicity about lawsuits in recent years, a large percentage of all negligence suits brought against psychiatrists, psychologists, and counselors continue to include claims of sexual misconduct. Clients who have been victims of such relationships clearly have the choice of filing ethical, administrative,[5] or legal complaints against their former counselors, and the resulting lawsuits may prove to be financially rewarding to certain clients. As cases in

---

the women ask for the information or their doctors believe an abortion is medically necessary.

[5]See for example, Johnson v. Board of Examiners in Psychology, 808 S.W.2d 766 (Ark. Sup. Ct. 1991); Friedman v. Board of Registration in Medicine, 561 N.E.2d 859 (Mass. Sup. Jud. Ct. 1990); Department of Professional Regulation v. Wise, 575 So. 2d 713 (Fla. Dist. Ct. App. 1991); Pundy v. Illinois Dep't of Professional Regulation, 570 N.E.2d 458 (Ill. App. 1991).

the area have risen, insurance companies now routinely exclude coverage for sexual misconduct, limit the damages that will be paid, or pay only for the legal defense of the counselor, but not for any damages that may be awarded (*St. Paul Fire & Marine Ins. Co. v. Love*, 1990).

Licensing statutes in many states also consider that sexual contact with clients or patients constitutes unprofessional conduct. For example, the Virginia statute, amended in 1994, includes in its definition of unprofessional conduct sexual contact with a patient at any time during the relationship *and* conduct of a sexual nature that a reasonable patient would consider lewd and offensive (Code of Virginia, §54.1-2914, 1994).

Claims of sexual misconduct by therapists have been based largely on the mishandling of the *transference phenomenon* and the countertransference that occurs when the therapist experiences reactions similar to their clients. Courts have found that the mishandling of this transference, resulting in sexual contact or touching, constitutes negligence or gross negligence for which damages can be awarded. Clients alleging sexual misconduct generally must prove in court that there was a counseling relationship, that sexual contact occurred between the counselor and the client, that the client suffered some emotional injury as a result of the contact, and in some states, that the contact occurred under the guise of treatment. In several states, however, a sexual relationship between a counselor and a client is sufficient grounds for a claim of negligence, whether it occurred under the guise of treatment or not. In order to ensure recovery from liability insurance carriers that may refuse to pay damages based on sexual misconduct, clients may allege other breaches of standard of care as well, such as boundary violations, failure to refer, premature termination of counseling, or other treatment diverging from the acceptable standard of care. The spouse or companion of a client who has engaged in sexual relations with a counselor also may bring a malpractice action and recover actual damages.[6] Attorneys who represent victims of alleged sexual misconduct now have a wealth of case law to guide them in securing damages for their clients, and there are few defenses available to the counselor who permits sexual contact in a therapeutic relationship.[7]

---

[6]See for example, Horak v. Biris, 130 Ill. App. 3d 140, 85 Ill. Dec. 599, 474 N.E.2d 13 (1985); Rowe v. Bennett, 514 A.2d 802 (Me. 1986); Figueiredo-Torres v. Nickel, 584 A.2d 69 (Md. Ct. App. 1991).

[7]The only defense that has consistently been effective once the act of sexual contact has been proved is that the suit is time-barred by the statute of limita-

Many of the reported cases of sexual misconduct involve psychiatrists and psychologists,[8] but counselors are not immune from suits in this area.[9] In fact, between 1987 and 1992 some 13% of the claims brought against counselors insured through the ACA Insurance Trust contained allegations of sexual misconduct. An analysis of claims between 1992 and 1994 reveal that this number may be increasing, and the more serious claims all fall in this area (Nelson, 1995). A case in Washington (*Doe v. Wood*, 1994) illustrates the danger to unwary counselors. A certified mental health counselor provided therapy to a couple and also socialized with them during the treatment period. The wife told her husband she had developed romantic feelings for the counselor, who later acknowledged the feelings were reciprocal. The counselor terminated the therapy. The husband later discovered letters from the counselor to the wife expressing his desire for a relationship with her. The couple separated, and the husband experienced a variety of symptoms of depression, emotional distress, and had difficulty working, resulting in a loss of income. He sued the counselor for professional negligence, intentional infliction of emotional distress, and outrage, claiming the counselor violated the standard of care by having a social relationship with the couple, pursuing a romantic relationship with the wife, betraying the patient's trust, and terminating the counseling relationship abruptly. The court awarded $525,000 on the professional negligence issue.

Counselors should keep in mind that they may also be held liable for the sexual misconduct of their colleagues or supervisees if they knew or should have known that such activity was occurring and failed to take steps to stop it. Is a colleague seeing a client at unusually late hours or away from the office? Does your supervisee lock his office door during sessions? Have any clients or co-workers complained or made remarks about the behavior of a supervisee? If so, as the employer or supervisor, you must take immediate steps to ensure compliance with the standards of care and protect the client(s) involved.

---

tions. Whether the client was competent to bring the action, and the actual final date of treatment or sexual activity, also are important in this determination.

[8]See, for example, New Mexico v. Leiding, 812 P.2d 797 (N.M. Ct. App. 1991); DiLeo v. Nugent, 592 A.2d 1126 (Md. Ct. Spec. App. 1991); MacClements v. LaFone, 408 S.E.2d 878 (N.C. Ct. App. 1991); and Doe v. Douglas County School Dist. RE-1, 770 F. Supp. 591 (D. Colo. 1991).

[9]See, for example, Sisson v. Seneca Mental Health/Mental Retardation Council, Inc., 404 S.E.2d 425 (W.Va. Sup. Ct. 1991); Doe v. Samaritan Counseling Center, 791 P.2d 344 (Alaska Sup. Ct. 1990); Poor v. Moore, 791 P.2d 1005 (Alaska Sup. Ct. 1990); Doe v. Wood, King County Sup. Ct. (Wash.), No. 93-2-00985-2, Aug. 12, 1994.

It is also important to remember that there may be criminal penalties from engaging in sexual relations with clients. Sentencing guidelines approved in Florida (Florida Rules, 1991), for example, refer to sexual misconduct with a psychotherapy patient as a criminal offense. Similarly, the Minnesota Court of Appeals has ruled (*Minnesota v. Ohrtman*, 1991) that it is a fourth-degree criminal offense for a psychotherapist to engage in sexual *contact* with a patient during a psychotherapy session. Further, the patient's consent does not constitute a defense to the action, the definition of "psychotherapist" includes the clergy, and "psychotherapy" by definition includes counseling.

The bottom line is that sexual contact between counselors and clients is ethically wrong, constitutes a breach of the standard of professional practice owed the client, causes actual harm to the client, and may violate criminal statutes as well. If you find yourself being drawn into a situation that could lead to such contact, you must keep the best interests of your client as your first priority. Refer the client to another therapist if appropriate. Terminate your relationship with the client in a timely manner. Seek consultation or supervision to ensure that the relationship remains open and professional, and secure the professional assistance you need to avoid mishandling the relationship with your client.

Nonclinical Issues

There are a variety of ways in which you can be held liable based on the actions of other practitioners, whether or not you have any control over their professional actions. The supervisor-supervisee relationship has been explored as one area of potential concern. Other situations can give rise to liability without the intent to assume such liability. Consider the common situation where several professionals share office space and perhaps clerical support. Because potential clients could easily mistake such relationships as partnerships, it is important to clarify the situation through a professional fact sheet or client information pamphlet. Credentials of the professionals practicing in the same location should be accurately and completely presented, together with an explanation of the professional affiliation (or lack of affiliation) for all employees and independent contractors.

Group Practice

Throughout the country, many independent professional counselors now share offices and overhead expenses, a practice that may expose them to increased risks of lawsuits based on the conduct of professionals over whom they have no control or responsibility. Some, in fact, have discontinued office sharing arrangements solely because of the threat of litigation. According to Moesel (April 1994), at least seven characteristics determine whether or not you are part of a group:

1. The group is considered a legal entity.
2. Clients see more than one counselor in an office.
3. Group members conduct joint sessions or seminars.
4. Your letterhead, billing statement, advertising, or office door sign shows more than one name.
5. Client records are stored together.
6. You share fees with other practitioners.
7. The public perceives you as a group.

If you are considered to be part of a group, whether or not you are an organized business entity, you may be held liable for the negligent acts of others in the group practice. You can minimize the risks by carefully checking out the references and licensing status of any other professionals who practice in your office and by applying for professional liability coverage as a group.

Alternatively, if you decide you want to maintain your separate and independent practice, be sure you clearly identify yourself as an independent contractor and establish that by maintaining separate billing accounts, letterhead, offices, and telephone numbers. Individual professional liability insurance should be purchased by all who share the office space.

Other Civil Actions

Dissatisfied clients may also pursue legal remedies against counselors for a variety of actions outside the traditional negligence or malpractice analysis. Frequently these claims will be coupled with a cause of action for malpractice or negligence, so it is important to understand the elements of each type of action.

Illegal Search and Seizure

The possibility for civil liability based on illegal search and seizure usually arises in a school or custodial setting and will most likely affect counselors who practice in those type of institutions. Counselors are likely to be involved with disciplinary matters in a school or institutional setting and may be asked to search either a student or resident or his room or locker storage areas. In so doing, counselors risk invading the resident's or student's constitutionally protected rights to privacy and to freedom from *unreasonable* search and seizure as set forth in the Fourth Amendment.

The Fourteenth Amendment extends this constitutional guarantee to searches and seizures by federal and state government officials and is enforced by means of the exclusionary rule, whereby evidence obtained as the result of an illegal search may not be used as evidence in a court of law (*Mapp v. Ohio*, 1961). If a counselor is asked to assist the police in conducting a search, either with or without a warrant, the counselor may follow reasonable orders and be free from fear of future legal action. The counselor in this setting is functioning only at the request of duly constituted authorities and presumably has not initiated the search.

Individuals' privacy rights also are guaranteed by the Constitution, and any "illegal search by a private individual is a trespass in violation of the right of privacy. . . . Any intentional invasion of, or interference with property, property rights, personal rights or personal liberties causing injury without just cause or excuse is an actionable tort" (*Sutherland v. Kroger Co.*, 1959). As a general rule, teachers or counselors have always been considered "private persons" in the jargon of search and seizure. The only "professional" recognized under the law was the law enforcement officer. As any other private person, counselors were not liable for an alleged illegal search of a pupil or resident so long as they were motivated by reasonable cause and acted with reasonable judgment, without malice, and with the best interests of the student or resident in mind. Consequently Fourth Amendment proscriptions generally did not apply to counselors, but they could be sued in tort for invasion of privacy unless these criteria were met.

In *New Jersey v. T.L.O.* (1985), however, the Supreme Court ruled that public school officials, including counselors, are instrumentalities of the state and are subject to the Fourth Amendment commands. As the Court wrote, "In carrying out searches and other disciplinary functions pursuant to such policies, school officials act as representatives of the State, not merely as surrogates for the parents, and they cannot claim the parents' immunity from the strictures of the Fourth Amendment."

Despite the fact that counselors and other public school and institutional administrators are "representatives of the state" and are therefore bound by the parameters of the Fourth Amendment, this does not mean that all searches are improper. Courts use a balancing of interests test to determine whether a search is "reasonable" according to the facts presented. As one court concluded, although a student "has a constitutional interest in freedom from governmental intrusion into his privacy . . . the State has an interest in educating children and to do so it is necessary to maintain order in and around the classroom" (*Interest of L.L.*, 1979).

The Supreme Court gave school officials broad powers to search students suspected of carrying weapons, dealing drugs, or violating other laws or school rules in the *New Jersey* case. Although the opinion adopts the position that the Fourth Amendment's prohibition on unreasonable searches and seizures applies to public school officials and that students have legitimate expectations of privacy, the Court also recognized that schools have an equally legitimate need to maintain a learning environment for all students. In order to meet this latter need, the Court ruled that the legality of a student search "should depend simply on the reasonableness, under all the circumstances, of the search." Whether a search is reasonable will depend on whether

> there are reasonable grounds for suspecting that the search will turn up evidence that the student has violated or is violating either the law or the rules of the school. Such a search will be permissible in its scope when the measures adopted are reasonably related to the objectives of the search and not excessively intrusive in light of the age and sex of the student and the nature of the infraction. (*New Jersey v. T.L.O.*, 1985)

School authorities, including counselors, stand in a unique position when it comes to searching school premises. Search warrants are unnecessary to access a student's locker or dormitory room so long as the official has "reasonable suspicion to believe" that illegal substances or items capable of undermining the order and good health of the school environment may be concealed there. Counselors are advised to avoid searches of students to the extent possible (including drug testing), but where this is not possible, counselors must be guided by a standard of reasonableness, as determined by all the facts of the case. A public high school policy of requiring all members of the band to submit to a search of their luggage prior to embarking on a concert trip was ruled unconstitutional by the Washington Supreme Court. Although the court recognized a statistical probability that some contraband would be found, because school officials lacked any reasonable information or belief that drugs or alcohol were hidden in the students' luggage, the search was impermissible (*Kuehn v. Renton School District No. 403*, 1985).

In June 1995 the U.S. Supreme Court again applied a balancing-of-interests test to uphold a local school board policy involving student searches in *Vernonia School Dist. v. Acton*, 1995). This case involved testing all student athletes' urine samples for illegal drugs at the beginning of each sport season and randomly throughout the season. Writing for the majority, Justice Scalia wrote:

> Fourth Amendment rights, no less than First and Fourteenth Amendment rights, are different in public schools than elsewhere; the "reasonableness" inquiry cannot disregard the schools' custodial and tutelary responsibility for children. For their own good and that of their classmates, public school children are routinely required to submit to various physical examinations, and to be vaccinated against various diseases. . . . Particularly with regard to medical examinations and procedures, therefore, "students within the school environment have a lesser expectation of privacy than members of the population generally" (*New Jersey v. T.L.O.* 469 U.S. at 348).

Justice Scalia went on to explain that privacy expectations of student athletes are even less than those of other students because of the communal showering, dressing, and changing in locker rooms that is required in sports participation. Further, student athletes voluntarily choose to play on a sports team, thus subjecting "themselves to a degree of regulation even higher than that imposed on students generally." Student athletes agree to comply with rules of conduct, dress, training hours, minimum grade point averages, and the like, so they "have reason to expect intrusions upon normal rights and privileges, including privacy."

Thus "having considered the scope of the legitimate expectation of privacy at issue here," the court balanced against that the nature of the intrusion caused by urinalysis drug testing. Because the conditions of the testing were similar to those men, women, and children typically encounter in public restrooms daily, the tests at issue look only for drugs and not other conditions of the body, the tests are reliable, and results are disclosed only to a limited number of school personnel and parents, the court ruled that the drug testing is reasonable in this case.

The Court went on to explain that the school board had an important—perhaps compelling—concern for deterring drug use among students of its schools, "for whom it has undertaken a special responsibility of care and direction." In view of these circumstances, the policy of the Vernonia, Oregon, school board is reasonable and constitutional, according to the Court. However, Justice Scalia cautioned that not all suspicionless drug testing will be appropriate. Each case must meet the test: Is the search one that a reasonable guardian and tutor might undertake?

Defamation

The tort action called *defamation* embodies the important public policy that each person should be free to enjoy his or her reputation unimpaired by false attacks, except in certain cases where a paramount public interest dictates that individuals be free to write or speak without fear of civil liability. Violations of this right form the basis for the action, which turns on whether the communication or publication tends, or is reasonably calculated, to cause harm to the reputation of another. In early common law this action was broken down into two separate actions: *slander*, a spoken or uttered word that defames a person; and *libel*, a defamatory writing. For most purposes today the two forms are treated as one action.

The key elements of a defamation suit brought by a private person are as follows:

1. The information complained of must be defamatory. That means the party must be exposed to hatred, ridicule, contempt, or pecuniary loss.
2. The information must have been communicated to someone other than the defamed person.
3. The defamed person must be alive.
4. The defamed person must have suffered some loss or injury as a result of the defamatory communication. In addition to obvious injuries such as loss of a job, honor, or award, damages for defamation may also be based on mental suffering and loss of reputation. Some states continue to recognize the common law action for slander in which a communication may be actionable if it
   a. Imputes to another the commission of a serious crime;
   b. Imputes that someone has a loathsome disease;
   c. Imputes a woman is unchaste; or
   d. Adversely affects someone's business, trade, or profession.

Counselors may be exposed to liability for defamation in the publication of records, letters of reference or recommendation, or in "loose talk" that may be untrue or damaging to the client as revealed to a third party. To avoid this, limits must be placed on written or verbal statements about clients. If the client can be identified from information provided in a conversation or a writing, even though the name is carefully withheld, the counselor may become the uncomfortable subject of a lawsuit as a result of that indiscretion.

The major defense to a defamation action is the truth of the statement or information communicated to the third party. In many states this is an absolute defense, just as in common law, although some states also require the statement to have been made in good faith and for a legitimate purpose. Absent some legitimate professional purpose, counselors who make even truthful statements about clients in those states could find themselves subjected to a defamation suit, just as for any other rumors or gossip.

The law also recognizes that in some situations the interests of the immediate participants or of society at large are so great that important, bona fide communications should be permitted freely without fear of resulting lawsuits. Except for the particular circumstances or occasion, as in a court of law, for example, the communication would be considered defamatory, but society's interest in promoting free communication outweighs the individual's concern for his or her reputation. Such privileges are granted by statute in almost all states for the proper discharge of official duties and are to be distinguished from the privileged communications discussed in Chapter 4 concerning confidentiality. In that discussion privilege was analyzed as a protection from revealing client confidences should a counselor be called to testify in court. This is a right that belongs to the client and binds the counselor to silence. When the term *privilege* is used in connection with defamation actions, it describes a privilege *to communicate*, which protects the counselor against money-damage defamation suits. The two privileges are not analogous.

Two types of communications are protected from defamation actions, those which are *absolutely privileged* and those which are *qualifiedly privileged*. Absolute privilege is based on the concept that the public interest in unimpeded communication in certain cases completely outweighs society's concern for an individual's reputation. Thus members of the legislature, judges, jurors, lawyers, and witnesses may speak freely in the exercise of their official functions without fear of civil suit. In fact, the Maryland Court of Appeals ruled that the comments of a psychologist, who recounted for a TV reporter the substance of his testimony during a custody hearing, were privileged on two counts. First, his testimony at the hearing was absolutely privileged. Second, the comments were privileged because they were merely reports of in-court testimony. Because the report was substantially accurate, the court ruled that it could not be actionable (*Rosenberg v. Helinski*, 1992).

Qualified privilege exists in situations where society's interest in unhampered communication is *conditionally limited* by the general mores as to what is fair and reasonable. Stated another way, based on their positions, certain individuals have a right to receive confidential reports or information that are not appropriate for publication to society at large. Generally, any statement made in a reasonable manner by one who is carrying out duties for a legitimate purpose will be protected by the qualified privilege. Counselors are frequently called upon in the course of their professional duties to make statements concerning clients to other people who have a corresponding duty or interest in receiving that information. For example, it might be necessary to inform a colleague or a parent that a client's difficulties stem from the use of illegal drugs or alcohol. A prospective employer may request general information about a client or seek specific information concerning ability or character in the course of conducting a security background investigation. Counselors may need to notify a social service agency of problems in a family to ensure the safety of a client. So long as such communications are made in good faith, with appropriate permissions or releases from the clients where needed, express only facts as known to the counselor, and are made only to persons having a proper interest in receiving the information, they will be protected.

Juries are commonly instructed to review five elements of communications to determine whether a qualified privilege exists:

1. The communication must be made in good faith.
2. It must promote an acceptable interest.
3. The statement is limited in scope to this purpose.
4. The occasions for transmittal must be proper.
5. Publication must be in a proper manner, and only to proper parties (*Owens v. Scott Publishing Co.*, 1955).

If all five conditions prevail, the communication will be considered privileged, and even a false statement will not be actionable in a defamation suit.

However, if the information is published improperly or excessively (through gossip, for example), or if the communication is maliciously motivated, the privilege will be lost and a court could find liability. *Malice* is defined legally as bad faith or action taken because of an unacceptable motive. Many jurisdictions hold that malice in the moral sense (hate, vindictiveness, animosity) need not be shown to forfeit the privilege. It is sufficient to show that a communication was made "without just cause or excuse" that is in "reckless disregard of the rights of others" (*Dunn & Bradstreet v. Robinson*, 1961). Using this standard, a court would consider whether the counselor had exercised sufficient care in ascertaining the truth of the information passed on to the third party.

In a libel action brought against a credit information company a jury awarded the plaintiff damages for injury to his reputation because false financial information was distributed to subscribers and the company made no attempt to correct the error. Because reporting credit information to subscribers created a conditional privilege, the plaintiff had to show that the credit company's actions were the result of malice. The court held that the negligence or carelessness of the credit company constituted malice because it amounted to conscious indifference and reckless disregard of the rights of the plaintiff. Counselors must also be cautious about client information disclosed to others. If false information is ever transmitted to a third party, corrections should be made as quickly as possible.

Counselors who act in a professional manner and are cautious about client information communicated to third parties will generally be protected from defamation actions by the qualified privilege. Here again, it is important to follow the ethical guidelines and obtain clear instructions and releases from clients, preferably in writing, detailing the information to be released.

Invasion of Privacy

Despite the truthfulness of a defamatory statement and the qualified immunity granted in the counseling situation, a counselor may still be held liable in an action for invasion of privacy if derogatory information is communicated to a third party who has no need or privilege to receive it. The action is based upon undue interference in the affairs of an individual through exposure or communication of his or her private affairs. The injury may result from truthful, but damaging, publications, and the person bringing the suit need not prove he or she has suffered any special injuries. In recent years concern about dissemination of computer records of personal and financial information has grown because of the potential for serious harm resulting from erroneous material. The problem is no less severe in the context of educational records and testing or in client records maintained in clinical practice. Counselors working in educational institutions should be thoroughly familiar with the requirements of the Family Educational Rights and Privacy Act (FERPA), or Buckley Amendment, discussed in Chapter 4, and take care to protect the student and family rights as set out.

Counselors employed in all fields are subject to potential liability for invasion of privacy if they administer educational or psychological tests without first fully informing the client of (1) the criteria to be used; (2) what skills or factors the test is designed to measure; (3) the possible uses of the test results; or (4) if they fail to explain test results. Some state laws now require testing agencies to provide various notices to test subjects and to disclose fully the factors outlined. The *ACA Code of Ethics* also admonishes counselors to obtain informed consent from clients prior to any assessment and further holds counselors responsible for using and interpreting competently any tests administered, and for releasing information only upon consent of the client, and then only to professionals who can competently interpret the results (E.2. and E.4.b.). Counselors should keep these criteria in mind when conducting testing and protect the written records of that testing accordingly.

The confidentiality of records also poses a problem for counselors because of concerns about invasion of privacy. The questions as to what should be included in a client or student record, and who might have access to that record, can generally be answered by the rules concerning defamation. First, reasonable care must be taken to ensure that the contents of records are accurate. A counselor who makes an entry designed to injure the client would run a serious risk of liability, even if the information were true. As noted, the reckless disregard of the rights of another can be sufficient to destroy the qualified privilege counselors enjoy in this area. Entering misleading or false information, or failing to make adequate corrections of such information, could meet this lower threshold definition of malice.

Second, the contents of records should be made known only to those who have a legitimate interest in them (for example, parents, professional colleagues, prospective employers) as defined by statute, regulation, or as established by a written release of information signed by the client or a parent of a minor client. These general rules are, of course, subject to more specific regulations or laws that may govern records in a particular state institution, agency, or school system. Counselors will not generally be held liable in a suit for invasion of privacy if required by law to disclose information or if the disclosure was not malicious and was made to serve certain overriding competing public interests, such as health regulations, reporting cases of abuse, or protecting a potential victim.

Breach of Contract

As noted in Chapter 3, counselors have certain duties arising from either express or implied contracts with clients. Express contracts usually are in writing, signed by the parties, and spell out the rights and responsibilities of each. Express contracts may be made orally and are just as binding on the parties, although proving the specific terms of the agreement may be difficult at some later time.

Implied contracts arise either through the relationship of the parties itself or as a result of actions of the parties that cause them to respond in a certain way or rely on each other. If a client comes to the counselor's office for a session each week at the same time and is charged a fee for services, which is paid, the parties will be held to have agreed to a contract that includes those terms. All these aspects of the relationship form the basis of the contract with the client, even though it is not expressly written. Should the counselor, absent some justification, fail to uphold his end of the bargain under the contract, the client can hold him responsible for breaching the contract. The counselor may be held liable for any damages suffered by the client as a result of that breach, including direct, incidental, and consequential damages (Lovett, 1980, n. 1).

Other considerations also may be viewed as terms of the counselor-client contract. It has been suggested that public knowledge of the ethical standards of the medical profession and the secrecy provisions of the Hippocratic Oath would be sufficient to justify a patient's belief that a physician must keep patient information confidential. Consequently, disclosure of such information might be treated as a breach of one of the implied terms of an implied contract between a physician and patient. To extrapolate from this theory, counselors are also bound by ethical standards and legal privileges protecting the confidentiality of client communications. A counselor also could be held liable for breaching an implied contract by disclosing information to others, as well as incurring tort liability for invasion of privacy or defamation.

Courts also may view professional advertising as terms of an express or implied contract with clients. For example, a firm or practice that advertises in a directory that they are *certified, licensed, registered, bonded,* or the like will be held to fulfill those terms or be found in breach of contract. Similarly, holding oneself out in advertising or client information brochures as an expert in any area also will bring increased responsibilities. Many states regulate the content of professional advertising in their licensing statutes, restricting the use of counseling titles and words such as "registered counselor" or "professional counselor." Along this line, deceptive or misleading advertising may simultaneously give rise to an action for violation of state deceptive or fraudulent advertising statutes.

Counselors should exercise care in all aspects of a client relationship, of course, but it is important to examine critically the whole spectrum of items that may form the basis of any contract with clients, whether express or implied. Written agreements detailing such items as the number and timing of sessions, fees, payment terms and information in the section on informed consent in Chapter 3 and in Appendix C will help to protect counselors. A counselor should never contract with a client concerning specific results or outcome of treatment, however, which may prove impossible to achieve.

Copyright Infringement

Original works that are published as articles, books, lectures, curricula, and the like are considered the intellectual property of their creators and are subject to the protection of federal and international copyright laws. This protection gives the copyright holder the exclusive right to print, publish, or otherwise reproduce the work, as well as to display and distribute copies, whether for free or for sale. Using protected material without permission is considered an infringement of the author's or publisher's rights and carries civil and criminal penalties.

Copyrighted material can be used properly by others in their own work as long as the fair use provisions of the Copyright Act of 1976 are followed, or if permission is secured from the copyright holder. The act sets out four factors to consider to determine *fair use:* (1) whether the material is used for commercial benefit or for non-profit educational purposes; (2) the medium of the work created; (3) how much of the work is used; and (4) the effect of using the work on the market and salability of the new work. With this in mind, quoting 5 or 10 lines from a research report in support of your findings in a clinical study, with proper attribution to the author, probably falls within the parameters of fair use. Even in that case it is prudent to request permission in advance. However, duplicating copies of an entire course syllabus, research study, or article for distribution to clients or students would infringe on the copyright protection and should not be done.

The widespread use of computers has proved of immeasurable benefit to counselors and administrators worldwide in recent years. Many agencies and institutions now commonly preserve counseling records and data on computer bases and use computers to facilitate client assessment and research. With the efficiency of this wonderful tool, however, a host of concerns have developed of which counselors should be aware. Many of these have been addressed in the *ACA Code of Ethics* and other professional ethical codes and relate primarily to the misuse of information or assessment tools. Other concerns relate to client misconceptions about computer assessment, counselor competence and training, accuracy of computer-based assessment programs, and the validity of test results.

Another important consideration for counselors who use computers for record keeping and testing is the application of federal copyright laws and licensing agreements. Most adults are aware of the general proscriptions against plagiarism and the protection for written and creative works offered by copyright laws discussed. Such protections also extend to computer operating programs and applications software in word processing, databases, assessment tools, and reporting. Applications software includes testing materials, scoring keys, normative tables, and report forms, according to the Eighth Circuit Court of Appeals. In *Regents of University of Minnesota v. Applied Innovations, Inc.* (1989) the court ruled that the development, reproduction, marketing, and distribution of software for scoring the Minnesota Multiphasic Personality Inventory (MMPI) infringed on the University of Minnesota's copyright of the test because it included copyrighted portions of the instrument. Obviously not all counselors are engaged in developing such scoring software, but this proscription applies to *users* of such programs as well.

It should be pointed out that "borrowing" computer programs and using bootlegged computer programs is an infringement on the rights of copyright holders and compromises the integrity of testing instruments. Such actions also deprive test and software creators of revenue to which they are legally entitled and, perhaps more important, they could lead to the promulgation of defective products that could adversely affect client treatment. Counselors are urged to comply with copyright laws and licensing agreements when they purchase computer software, just as they exercise care to comply with copyright laws in written or other materials.

Insurance Fraud

Strosnider and Grad (1993, p. 41) defined insurance fraud as "obtaining money from an insurance company by lies or deception." Although insurance companies may bring civil suits against service providers who misrepresent or misstate services in order to receive insurance reimbursements, insurance fraud may also be pursued by state licensing agencies and through criminal prosecution. All mental health service providers need to understand the specific provisions of insurance programs through which they seek payments and exercise care in complying with those provisions. Although this is a complex area, there are some specific practice recommendations to minimize the risk of liability for counselors.

First, counselors must render mental health diagnoses only for those they are qualified and competent to render under state licensing statutes. Report diagnosis codes accurately, and do not be persuaded to use an improper code to gain coverage. Be sure your client understands the full implications of any diagnosis you make and that once it is submitted to an insurance company it will become a part of her or his permanent health record.

Some insurance policies cover only individual psychotherapy sessions or cover individual sessions at a higher copayment rate than group counseling such as joint marital or family counseling. Be sure to investigate the terms of the particular policy your client is covered under and to use the appropriate codes for third-party billing, even though reimbursement may be limited or denied.

In submitting insurance claims, be careful to state the numbers and length of client visits accurately. Do not assume that four half-hour appointments in one week are the same to the insurance company as two one-hour appointments, particularly where the insurance company's responsibility for coverage is limited to two visits per week. Keep complete and accurate records of visits, and bill only for those you document.

The person who provides treatment must be the one to submit the insurance claim, even though consultants or supervisors may have been involved with the case. It is appropriate to note the names of supervisors or consultants, along with the name of the provider, but these should be clearly identified. This is especially important where an insurance policy covers therapy only when provided by a licensed psychiatrist, psychologist, or mental health counselor. Such services may not be reimbursed if provided by an intern or an unlicensed counselor, even though they may be working under the supervision of a licensed practitioner.

Finally, charging insurance companies for missed appointments, setting lower fees for clients without insurance coverage, or waiving copayments for clients are not appropriate.

Other Criminal Actions

Accessory to a Crime

Although counselors are honor bound to protect the integrity and promote the welfare of their clients, they also have an obligation to society at large that may override their duty to an individual client. The law makes it clear that any person who advises or encourages the commission of a crime can be charged as an accessory to the crime, even though the person took no active part in its commission. This is called *accessory before the fact*, and an individual convicted of such activity faces criminal penalties. The elements of the offense include: (1) evidence exists that the defendant in some way contributed to the crime by aiding or advising the alleged perpetrator; (2) the defendant was not present when the crime was committed; and (3) the alleged perpetrator is convicted of the crime or admits to it (*State v. Woods*, 1982).

However, merely concealing knowledge that a felony is to be committed does not make the party concealing it an accessory before the fact. So a counselor who learns from a client during counseling that a crime is to be committed may not have to reveal that knowledge to authorities, but counselors must be cautious in this gray area. Particularly in view of the *Tarasoff* decision (see Chapter 4), counselors must reach a balance between the confidential communications of a client and the need to preserve the safety and well-being of society. Although there is no hard and fast rule to follow, if you believe a client is about to commit a crime that would threaten the property, safety, health, or well-being of others, you have a duty to prevent the act from occurring. This is an active duty that may extend from attempting to discourage your client, to contacting local law enforcement authorities, depending on the circumstances of the case.

One thing should be made clear. A person need not personally participate in a criminal act to be charged as an accessory. Depending on the wording of your state laws, a counselor who learns that a client is about to steal or destroy property, sell or otherwise deal in illegal drugs, harm or injure another person, or supply information or paraphernalia that may assist someone else in committing a criminal offense can be held criminally liable as an accessory if he or she does not take adequate measures to prevent the offense.

A person who assists or aids a felon *after* a crime has been committed, knowing that the crime has been committed, may be similarly charged as an "accessory after the fact." An accessory after the fact is generally defined as "one who, knowing that a felony has been committed by another, receives, relieves, comforts or assists the felon, or in any manner aids him to escape arrest or punishment" (Criminal Law, §174). Three elements must be met:

1. A felony must have already been committed.

2. The person charged as an accessory must have knowledge that the person he or she is assisting committed the felony.
3. The accessory must harbor or assist the felon, intending to shield the felon from the law.

Evidence that a person helped to hide a felon, lent the felon money, gave advice, provided goods, offered transportation, blocked the path of pursuers, or gave false information tending to mislead authorities has been held sufficient to sustain a conviction as an accessory after the fact. It would be inaccurate, however, to say that *any* affirmative assistance or relief automatically results in charges that one has been an accessory. Even those acts just enumerated have not always been sufficient to justify conviction where there is no evidence that assistance was provided with the intention of harboring or assisting the felon.

You may recall how Al Cowlings came to the aid of O.J. Simpson after the 1994 murders of Nicole Brown Simpson and Ron Goldman. Although he was not prosecuted as an accessory, his actions certainly met the threshold test in that scenario. The law does not distinguish between a friend helping a friend, a business associate helping another business associate, or, for our purposes, a counselor aiding a client. The criminal prohibition is general in nature, and there is no exemption for counselors under the law. By applying the body of case law to the counseling situation, it is clear that a counselor who discovers that a client has committed a crime has an obligation to try to persuade the client to turn himself in to law enforcement authorities and must refrain from helping the client to hide from police.

Contributing to the Delinquency of a Minor

Although this topic is of primary concern to school counselors and those who work with families and children, others should be aware of the potential for contributing to the delinquency of minors and of the variety of acts that can trigger the offense. The majority of prosecutions for contributing to the delinquency of minors deal with people who patently attempt to subvert the morals of a juvenile. Even where such acts are unintentional, however, a counselor may not escape liability.

Contributing to the delinquency of a minor is not a common law offense. All states have enacted legislation of some form to protect children from any variation of the Fagin-Oliver Twist relationship (*State v. Crary*, 1959). Unfortunately not all state legislatures have defined the specific conduct that constitutes the crime, and many jurisdictions leave it to the jury to determine whether a defendant's conduct was criminal.[10] A broad definition of the offense might include any actions that tend to injure the health, morals, or welfare of juveniles or that encourage juveniles to participate in such actions. There is no certainty as to what constitutes this immoral conduct from state to state, however.

State courts also are divided on the question of intent. The traditional view is that a guilty intent, or *mens rea*, is a necessary element of the offense, but some states do not require *mens rea*. It is in these latter states that the danger of a counselor's inadvertently crossing the boundary of acceptable conduct is greatest. It is assumed that counselors would never deliberately do or encourage any act that would harm a minor. It is the inadvertent act, committed in the mistaken belief that it is legal, and more important, that it is in the best interest of the client, that causes concern. It is not possible in this book to analyze the laws of each state, so to avoid such liability counselors must research the law in the state(s) in which they practice and keep abreast of any changes in the statutes or cases that may occur.

[10]See Contributing to Delinquency, *Mens Rea*, 31 A.L.R.3d 848–867, for an in-depth study of the offense. See also 47 Am. Jur. 2d, Juvenile Courts, §63–69.

CHAPTER 6

MANAGING
YOUR COUNSELING
PRACTICE

L
ike other professionals, counselors must determine whether to
practice as employees, working for and under the direction of
someone else, an agency, or corporation, or whether to work in
private practice. This decision will be guided by a variety of
factors, especially the personality of the individual (including the extent to which he or she is willing to take risks), marital and family
status, financial circumstances, security needs, and professional preparation and experience. For some, the steady income and other security resulting from being employed by another is of paramount
importance. For others, the freedom to "be one's own boss" is the
overriding factor.

Professional counselors also face an array of choices, restrictions,
and possibilities determined by federal, state, and local laws and regulations. Those who choose to practice as employees of an institution
or counseling agency may be spared from complying with the resulting governmental requirements and forms that face employers, yet
employees, too, must meet certain reporting and filing obligations.
The purpose of this chapter is to provide some guidance about the
"business" aspects of both private and public professional counseling
practices. Please keep in mind that the material that follows is by necessity very general. It is intended to raise issues and questions for you
to consider. It is not designed as a substitute for the legal, business,
and financial planning professionals you should consult before making any decisions as you embark in private practice.

Form of Operation

Nonprofit Organizations

One of the threshold decisions in establishing a private counseling practice is whether to operate as a for-profit or nonprofit entity. Many services provided by the counseling profession can be (and are) housed in nonprofit organizations. This approach can offer a host of advantages, not the least of which is tax-exempt status, and the resulting ability to attract charitable gifts and donations and send mail at discounted rates.

To qualify for this preferential treatment, the programs of the organization must be within the bounds of what is considered charitable, educational, or scientific activities within the scope of section 501(c)(3) or 501(c)(4) of the Internal Revenue Code. This form is probably most appropriate if the counselor is motivated less by the objective of building a business and more by the prospect of operating a program that emphasizes research, publications, seminars, or the provision of certain types of counseling services. A counselor may "own" a nonprofit entity in the sense of controlling its board of directors. Further, a counselor who is an employee may receive a reasonable salary, and an independent contractor may also receive reasonable payments for services rendered to a nonprofit organization.

Generally speaking, a nonprofit entity must qualify for tax-exempt status under federal tax law. Once that is accomplished, there is probably a similar exemption under state law as well. The privileges of tax exemption come at a price, however, including limitations on lobbying and political activities and annual informational returns that must be filed by most exempt organizations with the Internal Revenue Service.

For-Profit Entities

Although many practices are incorporated, this is by no means mandatory. For many years small businesses have operated successfully as unincorporated, sole proprietorships. Of course, where two or more counselors are in the same practice, the alternative to incorporating may be to form a partnership. Again, whether one practices alone or as part of a group is a matter that involves personality and economic circumstances, rather than simply considerations of law. But whether one chooses to operate a counseling practice in one business form rather than another is very much dictated by legal considerations.

A chief determinant is the avoidance of personal liability. Forming a corporation shields the individual owners, directors, officers, or employees of the corporation from personal liability for acts arising out of its business operations because it is a separate legal entity. If creditors or others (clients) initiate lawsuits against the corporation, the private assets of the individual officers, directors, or employees will usually be immune from their reach. This would include, for example, claims for breach of contract, uncollected debts, false or misleading advertising, nonpayment of taxes, accidents that occur on the premises, and other similar situations. Although negligence and malpractice claims that may be brought against individual employees are usually also filed against the counseling service or agency that employs them, the owners, officers, directors, and employees of that corporate entity would be protected or shielded from personal liability by the corporation. As a result, although banks and other financial institutions make loans to small businesses, in the case of closely held corporations, they will usually require owners, directors, or officers to give a personal guarantee or bond that the loan and interest will be paid.

The perceived exposure to personal liability, federal and state tax considerations, and the stringencies of creating and maintaining a corporation, partnership, or other entity under your state's law are likely to be the principal factors in choosing the business form for your practice. Also, if counseling services are to be provided in one or more additional states, your counseling entity will probably have to register or "qualify" in the other jurisdictions in order to conduct business as a "foreign corporation."

It is important to stress that incorporation is not mandatory or advisable in all situations. The initial costs of incorporation and attendant filing fees are not substantial, but the continuing formalities necessary to maintain the corporation may prove onerous. These include separating the financial records of shareholders and the corporation, holding regular meetings of shareholders and directors, issuing stock and maintaining stock transfer records, and filing annual reports. Further, the advantage offered corporations by limited liability only applies so long as the corporate formalities are preserved. Failure to adhere to these formalities, particularly regarding commingling of funds and filing required reports, can lead to loss of corporate status and thus loss of protection against personal liability.

In some states, if the corporate form is selected, a counseling practice may be set up as a "professional corporation," rather than organized as a standard business corporation. This may offer additional benefits, or reduced reporting, depending on the rules in your state. Another possibility to consider is the subchapter S corporation. A federal tax law option, the S corporation allows an enterprise to be created as a corporation under state law, thereby preserving the shield against personal liability, yet be treated as a partnership for federal tax law purposes. This means that the tax deductions and tax credits experienced by corporations are not frozen at the corporate level but are passed along to the stockholders in their personal capacities.

Mostly in response to the federal tax creation of the subchapter S corporation, some states have recently established a similar entity in the form of the *limited liability company* (LLC). Like the subchapter S corporation, the LLC achieves a limited liability for owners similar to that of a stockholder of a corporation while permitting partnership-style pass-through treatment of income for tax purposes. There are no particular limitations set on who may be a member of an LLC, flexibility of allocating income, losses and cash flow is permitted, and the strict qualification rules of the subchapter S corporations do not apply. There are, however, some disadvantages to this entity, mostly arising from the uncertainty about how jurisdictions that do not recognize LLCs deal with them.

Operating Instruments and Organizational Meeting

Regardless of which organizational form is chosen, business entities are governed by the operating instruments by which they are created and that state their operational rules. For a corporation, the creating document is its *articles of incorporation*, the contents and form of which are usually dictated by state law. The corporation's operating rules are contained in its *bylaws*. For a partnership, the creating document is the *partnership agreement*, which usually includes the general operational rules, although a set of bylaws or other rules may be developed to guide its day-to-day management. Limited liability companies are created by articles of organization and governed by an operating agreement that is a combination of partnership agreement, limited partnership agreement, and corporate bylaws.

When forming a business entity, you must observe a number of organizational formalities. First among these is the organizational meeting, with its proceedings recorded in minutes. Depending on the rules in your state, a variety of actions may occur at this meeting, including selecting and approving the organizational structure, authorizing bank accounts, and retaining a lawyer and accountant. Corporate rules also may require an initial meeting of the corporation where directors other than those listed in the articles of incorporation may be elected, together with the corporation's officers.

Business Procedures

Once your professional practice has been formally established either as a corporation, partnership, subchapter S corporation, LLC, or sole proprietorship it is vitally important that a variety of business procedures be implemented to ensure your practice is conducted in a professional manner. Consideration must be given to financial accounting and tax recording and filing systems, contracts for lease or purchase of property and office equipment and furnishings, employees, insurance for the practice, premises and employees, advertising, systems for filing claims for reimbursement with insurance companies, continuing education programs, colleagues and supervisors, and the like. Your financial and legal advisors will be able to assist with specific recommendations, but there also are a variety of service organizations that offer general business advice. It is just as important to be prepared for the business aspects of your practice as it is to be competent to offer counseling services to the public.

Insurance Protection

Once you have established the location of your office and purchased or leased furnishings and equipment, it is important to consider a variety of insurance protection policies to minimize your risk of unprotected or insufficiently compensated losses. A competent insurance agent or broker can help to demystify some of the complexities of policy contracts and coverage, but it is important for you to read such documents thoroughly and be sure that both you and the agent or broker understand the nature of your professional practice and the scope of coverage and exclusions provided. Once established, insurance policies should be reviewed every year to be sure conditions have not changed.

The description of types of insurance coverage that follows is intentionally general, but should give counselors an overview of the types of policies available. Professional liability coverage is reviewed later in this chapter and is therefore omitted from this discussion. Before you contract for any insurance coverage, be sure to investigate thoroughly the rating, business reputation, and claims procedures of the underwriting company.

General liability insurance is usually written as a comprehensive policy that protects your *practice* from legal liability for losses associated with the premises and operations, contracts, administrative errors, actions of officers and directors or employees, fire, flood, third-party medical expenses, personal injury, nonowned automobiles, and the like. The insurer's total liability to cover losses will be stated on the declarations page and will usually include a single limit for the majority of coverage. The comprehensive policy may also include workers' compensation and coverage for uninsured or underinsured motorists' protection. Policies vary widely, as do premiums for coverage, so counselors are advised to consult with several insurers to compare coverage and costs.

Property insurance will cover your practice's *real or personal property, or interest in rental property* from losses from multiple risks. These include fire, lightning, windstorm, or other acts of God, smoke, vandalism, malicious mischief, and so on. Coverage also is available for accounts receivable, office equipment, computers, electronic media, signs, fixtures, landscaping, fine arts, and the like that many practices may use in the course of business. It is recommended that a complete inventory of all real and personal property in which your practice has an interest be conducted annually to determine the adequate protection required through the property insurance policy. Some items to consider when reviewing policies include whether coverage is provided for: (1) *replacement cost* of items lost or damaged, including improvements you have made to the premises; (2) lost rents/income; (3) debris removal; (4) temporary quarters and equipment rental; and (5) lost earnings and extra expenses due to temporary relocation. Does the policy provide for automatic increases of property limits? Is coverage based on replacement rather than on actual cash value? Will the replacement cost be paid regardless of whether the property is actually replaced? Each of these can result in a substantial benefit to your practice in the event of a covered loss.

Surety and fidelity bonds generally cover the risks associated with the dishonesty and performance failure of employees, officers, and directors. The bonding or insurance company agrees to pay a third party for any losses that are the result of acts or negligence of their insured (i.e., your professional practice). This would cover the acts of all employees, whether professional or nonprofessional, and includes fraud, dishonesty, disappearance, and destruction. Such coverage may also be included in a comprehensive general liability policy, so you should examine the terms carefully to avoid duplication.

One risk associated with professional practice that many practitioners in all professions overlook is *business overhead expense cover-*

age. If one or more of the key partners or officers of a small counseling practice becomes disabled, the risk of financial ruin is great. If two counselors share all the overhead expenses of their practice and one becomes seriously ill or is injured, the expenses of continuing operations may force the closing or discontinuation of the practice because of the extent of financial commitments of salaries, rents, and utilities. Purchasing business overhead expense coverage can protect from this exposure by covering general overhead expenses for limited periods of time.

Private practitioners also need to consider employee benefit programs. *Group medical benefits, hospitalization, life, and income-replacement (disability) programs* are designed to protect employees and their families from the expenses of illness or injury and can help to attract and retain good employees. However, the costs can be high. Furthermore, such coverage is not required by law, and numerous federal and state laws make providing medical benefits very complex.

Your review of employee medical benefit programs should include a discussion of what benefits are to be provided, the amount the professional practice can afford to contribute, and whether employees will contribute to the amount paid by the firm, as well as the deductibles, basic benefit levels, limits of coverage, co-insurance percentages, and similar requirements of the policy. As the impact of managed care, health maintenance organizations, preferred provider organizations, and other alternate health care management structures is getting stronger, providing medical benefits coverage is both complicated and expensive. Counselors need to examine a variety of programs and plans to determine what form will best meet the needs of their practice and employees.

Disability income protection is designed to replace the individual professional counselor's income in the event of a long-term illness or accident that restricts his or her ability to continue to practice and earn a living. These policies are available for both long and short terms, although long-term policies are widely regarded as the most critical. Short-term illnesses can usually be covered by personal investments or other sources, but those sources are quickly exhausted by a long-term illness. Insurers will usually underwrite only a percentage of an individual's annual earnings from professional practice, and how the premiums are paid may affect the individual's tax situation, so it is wise to consult with both the employee and tax advisers at the time the policy is purchased.

Finally, *group life insurance* is contained in almost all employee benefit programs, frequently as part of a group medical plan. Term life insurance is the least costly to obtain on a group basis, and it may be convertible to permanent forms of insurance to provide security for employees who leave your employ. Providing a reasonable level of low-cost protection should be the primary goal of your program, but keep in mind that policy provisions may vary widely in benefits, conditions, eligibility, and exclusions and should be examined closely.

Federal and State Taxes and Reporting

Federal, state, and some local governments require that businesses submit a variety of annual information and tax returns. Your local Internal Revenue Service office (call the toll-free tax information telephone line listed in the telephone directory), state office of taxation, or a local government office should be able to provide you with the necessary information booklets and blank forms that must be filed for business licenses, state and local employee taxes, unemployment taxes, real and personal property taxes, and business income taxes, among others. Your lawyer or accountant can also help to determine which reports and forms are required and when and where they must be filed.

Employment Law Considerations

Employment law is also becoming more complex in the wake of civil rights protections, sexual harassment cases, and even the legal ramifications of giving references for former employees. Here again, it is beyond the scope of this work to give a comprehensive discussion of the law in this area. A good discussion of employment discrimination and sexual harassment is contained in *Law and Management of a Counseling Agency or Private Practice* (Bullis, 1993). But this is an area of law that changes rapidly and can trap an unwary counselor faced with hiring or termination decisions. The information that follows is a bare-bones sketch of the employment process, some of the proscriptions that may apply, and recommendations for your private practice.

Employment Discrimination

Before you consider hiring your first employee, be sure to learn all you can about employment discrimination laws that may affect your practice. These laws apply to all aspects of employment, from position announcements, applications, interviews, and testing to terminations and must be followed closely.

Title VII of the Civil Rights Act of 1964 (Title VII) is the federal statute that forbids employment discrimination based on race, color, sex (including pregnancy), national origin, or religion. It applies to federal, state, and local government employers and to private employers with more than 15 employees if their business "affects interstate commerce." This has been broadly interpreted to include activities conducted in other states, such as consulting, speaking engagements, teaching, or conferences, so even a small private counseling service may find that its activities must comply with federal and various state employment laws. It is clear that Title VII applies to counselors working in state and federal agencies, colleges, and universities. Even though your small private agency may have fewer that 15 employees, and therefore is not technically subject to the federal statute, the policies embodied in the law are good guidelines to follow with employees and may help you to avoid other problems later. Furthermore, many states have similar employment discrimination laws that apply to all employers within the state.

Title VII provides for enforcement by the Equal Employment Opportunity Commission (EEOC), which is initiated by filing charges within 180 days of the alleged discriminatory act. In some areas charges must be filed with a local civil rights agency within 300 days of the alleged discrimination. The EEOC has the power to investigate any such claims, to seek conciliation, or to bring suit against the employer. If the EEOC decides not to bring an action against the employer in court, notice is given that the original complainant has the right to sue the employer within 90 days. The remedies available to a successful complainant include back pay, injunctive relief (such as an order to rehire, reinstate, or promote the employee), reasonable attorney's and expert fees, as well as compensatory (for intentional discrimination) and punitive damages (upon a showing of malice or "reckless indifference").

Other federal laws also affect employment, including the Equal Pay Act of 1963, which requires men and women to be compensated equally for equal work. This applies to jobs that involve equal skill, effort, and responsibility and are performed under similar working conditions in the same establishment, although "equal work" need not be identical work (*Corning Glass Works v. Brennan*, 1974). Furthermore, the discrimination need not be intentional, and the Act covers most private employers and state and local governments.

The Age Discrimination in Employment Act of 1967 (ADEA), protects employees age 40 and older against employment discrimination based on age and includes mandatory retirement in most cases.

The ADEA applies to employers with 20 or more employees, labor unions, employment agencies, and their agents. The ADEA is also enforced through the EEOC according to the enforcement scheme established for violations of Title VII.

The Family and Medical Leave Act of 1993 requires covered employers (with at least 50 employees within 75 miles) to provide up to 12 weeks of unpaid, job-protected leave to eligible employees (who have worked for at least 1 year or at least 1,250 hours over the previous 12 months) for certain family and medical reasons. The employer must maintain the employee's group health coverage for the duration of the leave, and using such leave cannot result in the loss of any employment benefit that had accrued prior to the start of the employee's leave.

The Immigration Reform and Control Act of 1986 prohibits discrimination on the basis of national origin or citizenship, except against unauthorized aliens.

The Americans With Disabilities Act of 1990, discussed in greater length later in this chapter, prohibits discrimination against qualified individuals who have a disability. It requires employers to make reasonable accommodations to the conditions of qualified individuals with disabilities and is enforced according to the administrative scheme set out in Title VII. However, if the employer can show he or she made a good faith effort to make reasonable accommodations, compensatory and punitive damages are not available.

State Nondiscrimination Statutes

Investigate state and local laws concerning discrimination that may be broader than the federal statutes. Even though your practice may fall outside the scope of the federal statutes, you may be subject to state regulations.

Sexual Harassment

Establish a comprehensive antiharassment policy for your counseling practice and communicate it to all staff members, whether professional or nonprofessional employees. Make sure they understand that employers "have a duty to provide a workplace that is free from sexual harassment and to protect employees from unwanted, unwelcome sexual overtures and invitations of a sexual nature whether such conduct originates with partners in the firm, associates, fellow employees, clients or outsiders" (Coleman, 1995, p. 39).

Recruiting, Hiring, and Managing Employees

As you prepare to recruit and hire your first employees, and once they begin their employment, you should address several items (the following material was adapted with permission from Anderson, 1994):

- Establish job descriptions for all proposed employees, set minimum criteria for skills and competencies for each position, and determine job performance standards.
- Establish general employment policies for recruiting, screening, hiring, and managing employees, performance reviews, compensation, work hours, vacations, leave, discipline, and termination of employment. Be sure to preserve your rights as employer to modify any personnel policies without prior notification and, where permitted by state law, to terminate employment at any time with or without cause. Review these policies with your business attorney.
- Be sure you understand what types of questions are permissible when interviewing candidates for employment. If you are not aware of potentially discriminatory questions, consult your attorney, the EEOC, the Small Business Administration, or your state's employment commission for information.
- Establish and maintain personnel files on all employees. Retain copies of applications, letters of recommendation, federal, state, and local tax information, annual performance reviews, and the like, along with general salary and benefits information.
- Document personnel files with any incidents of substandard performance, violations of employer policies, or other misconduct. Consider whether any discipline decision is appropriate. Consult with a supervisor, personnel manager, or other management official where possible. If it should become necessary to discharge an employee, do not provide written reasons for termination unless required by contract. Document your files, however, with the problems and reasons for termination. Finally, treat the employee with respect. Give actual reasons for termination clearly; do not argue with the employee; and arrange for a time to discuss final business matters such as accrued vacation, severance, retirement, and other benefits rights.
- Protect the privacy rights of your employees and former employees. Develop and follow a policy for references for terminated employees. You are free to release to others the fact and dates of employment. If your former employee wants additional

information disclosed, however, secure a written release from the employee that specifies the information to be disclosed and to whom. Retain this release with the employee's personnel record. Be careful not to disclose highly sensitive information about employees or their families, particularly medical information. Employers certainly have the right to information needed to determine the fitness of a candidate for employment, but this must be balanced against the employee's right of privacy.

Employment Contracts

You may be in a situation where a contract of employment is desirable or required to practice as part of the professional counseling firm or agency. Most states recognize and enforce reasonable clauses and covenants contained in employment contracts, even though they may follow the law of "at-will" termination of employment in other cases. There are two types of clauses that frequently are included in such contracts of which you should be aware.

The first is a *hold harmless* clause, in which the employee counselor agrees to accept all liability from any and all lawsuits that may result from his or her professional actions. Two theories of law permit employers of counseling professionals to be held liable for the negligent acts of their employees. The first is the concept of *respondeat superior* (the Latin phrase means "let the master answer"), or *vicarious liability*. In the typical case a dissatisfied client files a negligence or malpractice action against the counselor who failed to improve the client's condition *and* against the counseling agency or service that employs her. The counseling service is presumed to have deeper pockets than the individual counselor, thus enhancing the chances of recovering on any award.

The second theory is that the counselor is acting as the *agent* for his supervisor or employer, who is the *principal*. The law of agency is far more complicated than this, but essentially the agent works on behalf of the principal, having a legal duty to do so, and can bind the principal through his actions. In both cases, the employer may be held responsible for the actions of the employee, even though he did not specifically consent to the act complained of or agree to accept liability.

The hold harmless clause changes the equation by shifting the financial responsibility for negligent acts of the employee back to the employee. Thus although both the counselor and the counseling service in the negligence action described may be held legally liable for the counselor's breach of duty, the counselor may be required to reimburse the service for the costs of defending the lawsuit based on the provisions of the hold harmless clause in her or his employment contract. Such clauses certainly are not mandatory, but they do offer protection to the employer and are a point for negotiation.

The second type of restrictive clause that frequently finds its way into employment contracts is the *covenant against competition, or covenant not to compete.* Generally such clauses restrict employees from leaving a firm or practice and opening up a competing professional practice in the same vicinity for some period of time. So long as the clause is not broader than is reasonably necessary to protect the legitimate interests of the employer, and it relates directly to the specific duties of the former employee, courts will usually uphold such agreements. Similar clauses restricting former employees from soliciting the clients of the former employer are also frequently upheld.

Hiring, Training, and Supervising Employees

As employers, counselors have a variety of responsibilities to their employees and to their clients that arise from the *respondeat superior* theory described. To the extent they exercise control over employee conduct, employers may be held accountable for resulting actions, even though they did not intend for those acts to occur (*Doe v. Samaritan Counseling Center*, 1990). Following the negligence theory of *respondeat superior*, some courts have allowed recoveries against employers on the basis of negligent hiring, retention, supervision, and training of employees. In these cases the negligence analysis discussed in Chapter 5 is used to determine whether employers should be held liable for damages caused by their employees. Was there a foreseeable risk that could have been avoided if the employer had not neglected his or her duty? Was the act complained of within the scope of the employment? Could reasonable training, whether pre-employment or in-service, have averted or minimized the risk? For more information on the scope of these theories, counselors are advised to consult Bullis (1993) and their legal counsel. Be advised that employers are also responsible for the acts of volunteers, students, and supervisees working in a counseling service, and these individuals should be held to the same standards of conduct as employees. The material that follows generally applies to volunteers, students, and supervisees, as well as to employees.

There are ways to minimize employer exposure to liability for the acts of employees. Certainly, a hold harmless clause in an employment contract and liability insurance coverage are two possibilities. Your affirmative efforts to diminish the risks at the outset may prove more effective, however, and these should include the following:

- Always check the references and backgrounds of applicants for employment for any position within your firm. If the applicant is a mental health professional, be sure to contact the state licensing board to ascertain his current licensure status. Require all applicants to provide certified original copies of transcripts and licenses. Call or write to previous employers to verify employment status and dates and ask about the applicant's job responsibilities and performance while he or she was employed there.
- Be sure applicants for employment have the required professional degrees and preparation (including licensure, certification, or registration) to ensure competence. Discuss treatment theories and concepts with a professional applicant to determine for yourself that the applicant is competent to treat *your* clients.
- Require your employees (both professional and nonprofessional) to participate in in-service training and professional development. Membership in professional associations and adherence to professional ethical standards should be encouraged.
- Discuss the internal policies and procedures of your agency or counseling service with your employees. Be sure that all employees understand the nature of the counselor-client relationship and the need for strict confidentiality of client information. Explain carefully that their continued employment depends on strict adherence to all employment policies, including rules concerning behavior and conduct with clients.
- Be alert to changes in employee behavior or erratic performance. Are unusual noises coming from one office during counseling sessions? Is a counselor meeting a client after hours? Is that counselor's door locked during some appointments? Have other employees or clients commented on the strange behavior of an employee? Any of these signals that further investigation is needed immediately.
- If you are serving as a supervisor or consultant to another counselor, whether or not he or she is your employee, schedule regular meetings to discuss case management. Be sure to allow enough time to discuss adequately the case and treatment being provided. Remind the supervisee of the continuing need to protect client confidences, and determine whether the client is aware

of the supervision or consultation. Check back with the supervisee at regular intervals to determine if expected progress is being made.

- If you become aware that an employee, particularly a mental health professional, needs additional training to become competent in a new specialty area or to manage a particularly difficult case (if referral is not appropriate for some reason), schedule in-service training, bring in an outside consultant, or find a training course or seminar that will satisfy that need.

Records and Record Keeping

Well-organized and well-documented client counseling records are the most effective tool counselors have for establishing client treatment plans, ensuring continuity of care in the event of your absence, proving that quality care was provided, justifying reimbursement of fees for services, establishing reliable information for decision making in court cases where difficult issues are presented, and for avoiding malpractice liability. With the growth of managed care, counselors must carefully document their services to ensure reimbursement under health plans. In fact, according to some practitioners, the importance of records continues to grow with "the amount of organization, the use of objective pre- and post-treatment measures and more emphasis placed on treatment planning between sessions" (R.E. McCarthy, quoted in Marino, 1995).

Unfortunately, the methodology and importance of clinical and business records are not taught in counselor education courses and many counselors are unaware of the ramifications of poor documentation. Most states require counselors to keep counseling records and a variety of mental health professionals have had their licenses suspended for failing to maintain proper documentation (*Camperlengo v. Barell*, 1991; see also *Suslovich v. New York Educ. Dep't*, 1991). In fact, the failure to maintain adequate client records could form the basis of a claim of professional malpractice because it breaches the standard of care expected of a practicing mental health professional. If you have stated treatment options in a patient record, documented that you consulted with another professional colleague, recorded your decision, and supported it with reasons, you will be in a good position to defend yourself from a future claim of malpractice. Even though you made the wrong decision, it would be difficult to prove you neglected the standard of care in that scenario. So it is important to keep accurate and complete records on all clients.

Your records belong to you, but the information contained in those records belongs to the client. You have an obligation to protect the confidentiality of client records, as discussed in Chapter 4, but you should always operate under the assumption that a variety of individuals may at some time have access to your records, including professional colleagues, insurance companies, attorneys, courts, and your client. Some believe that clients and patients should take an active part in reading and helping to write their records. Not only does this practice reassure clients about the content of counseling records, but it also helps to ensure that they understood the counseling session, makes them more involved with their therapy, and may help to avoid malpractice suits based on client dissatisfaction (Mitchell, 1991).

Notwithstanding ethical confidentiality concerns, the contents of counseling records may be discoverable by a court of law, inspected by insurance companies, and released to others upon waiver by your client, so you must ensure that your record keeping is complete, accurate, and free of any extraneous materials that could prove embarrassing at some later time. Notes in the margins, telephone numbers casually jotted down on the back of a record, and "doodles" have no place in client records. Personal criticism of your client in progress notes could be extremely embarrassing at some later date.

Evidence of "whiteout," erasures, crossed-out notes, and notes out of sequence, reflect changes and alterations and could lead someone reading your records to believe you are disorganized and perhaps less than honest. All notations should be made contemporaneously, not constructed after the fact, and particularly not *after* you receive a subpoena. It is also important never to change or alter records so they "look" better before you must release them.

The "personal notes" of a counselor, if kept separate from the client's records, generally will not be discoverable. However, it will require you to maintain two completely separate sets of records on clients or patients, which may prove to be impossible on a regular basis. Notes you keep of conversations with your legal counsel also should be kept separate from the client's files.

Your state licensing statute may set minimum standards for the content of counseling records. If you work in an agency, counseling service, university, or college, it is likely that your employer has policies on maintaining client records. These might include the content of client records (plan, progress notes, etc.), format and style of notes, the need for clarity and common vocabulary among agency staff, and who is to respond to outside inquiries for client information. Good examples of the content and form of client records can be found in *Documentation in Counseling Records* (Mitchell, 1991). At the very minimum, a client record should include the name, address, and telephone number of the client and of the responsible billing party. A signed copy of an informed consent form, if you use one, any correspondence from or about the client, and any waivers or releases of confidentiality signed by the client should also stay with the record. The client's history and testing information, notations of the dates and services provided, progress notes, or other notes from other professionals should be included in the file as well. Be sure your notes document all your efforts to treat the client's problem(s) and your reasons for choosing one treatment method over another. Keep in mind that when you are away from the office, another counselor may need to use your notes and other information from the client's record to be able to help one of your clients. Records must be complete and accurate to meet that need.

Financial records should also be maintained on all clients to assist in seeking reimbursement from insurance and other health plans and to document the financial relationship. Whether these records should be kept with counseling records is a matter for individual consideration. Many practices have separate billing departments that handle financial matters, and counselors have limited, if any, contact with fees and collections. There should be some mechanism, even in larger firms, however, to inform a counselor if a client is delinquent in paying for services. There may be other underlying problems of which the counselor should be aware, and the counselor should encourage the client to meet this obligation promptly.

Many counseling agencies now maintain client records, schedules, and financial information on computers. This medium certainly helps to eliminate paperwork and saves time, but there are some potential problems. First and foremost, authenticating the content and dates of records may be difficult with electronic media designed to be flexible and maneuverable. Be sure to include dates of entries in computer records, and establish procedures to ensure security of access to computer files. Also important is to implement a plan for frequent backup of information to avoid losing files if a computer crashes (or the computer operator accidently erases information).

Finally, if one is not already in place, establish a records retention policy for your firm, agency, or practice. If your state licensing statute provides guidance on retaining client records, be sure to follow it carefully. Determine the relevant statutes of limitations in your state to assess how long you should keep client records. Although they recognize that some authorities recommend keeping all client records indefinitely, Bertram and Wheeler (1994) suggest keeping records for at least 7 years. All client records should be kept, not just some of the records, and how those records will be maintained should be determined (i.e., microfilm, microfiche, computer disks, boxed files). Also determine where records will be stored to keep them safe and secure, and how and when they will be destroyed. Last, but not least, you should appoint a records custodian to retain counseling records in the event of your death or disability. This will be of little concern to counselors who practice in large services or agencies, but for small practices, it is important that a trusted professional colleague be appointed the caretaker of your client records.

Third-Party Payments

The insurance field is changing rapidly in this country with the advent of managed care, preferred provider organizations, and health maintenance organizations, as well as among the traditional insurance carriers. As medical costs rise, and as the state and federal governments try to grapple with deficits, we will see further changes in the next few years. To provide the greatest assistance to clients, professional counselors must become as knowledgeable of health care issues as possible and must actively work to educate carriers and health care administrators about their competence and the scope of professional services they provide. Counselors also should learn about the statutes in the states in which they practice that apply to insurance reimbursement, including obtaining and keeping copies of state-mandated benefits and antidiscrimination laws.

Some insurance carriers limit their coverage to medical providers and are reluctant to provide reimbursement for the services of a professional counselor. In such cases you may have to persuade the carrier that reimbursement for counseling sessions is appropriate based on the academic and clinical preparation, certification and licensing of professional counselors, and is in the best interest of the client. Glosoff (1993) suggests preparing a fact sheet about both licensed professional counselors and your own professional preparation and sending that to reluctant carriers with copies of state licensing statutes and of national certifications.

As you prepare to submit claims for reimbursement on behalf of clients, there are several items to consider to make the claims process operate smoothly and to prevent potential legal problems:

- Establish procedures in your office for completing and filing claim forms promptly. Do not let claims pile up. Get complete insurance information from each client, including policy numbers, employer authorization numbers, and claim procedures. Be sure all claims filed are complete and accurate, including the signature of the provider.
- Obtain the proper insurance claim forms, such as the HCFA-1500.
- Know and use the appropriate (and most recent) diagnostic codes (DSM-IV, from the *Diagnostic and Statistical Manual of Mental Disorders* [APA, 1994], and ICD, from the *International Statistical Classification of Diseases and Related Health Problems* [WHO, 1994]). and procedural codes (CPT, from the *Physicians Current Procedural Terminology* [American Medical Association, 1995]).
- Be sure to state all services you provide accurately and completely. The frequency and duration of sessions, as well as correct diagnosis codes, should be stated factually, not embellished for purposes of securing reimbursement.
- Keep accurate records of counseling sessions and of reimbursement requests submitted. Be sure your records support the claims you file in the event of a claims review or audit.
- Do not bill carriers for missed appointments or charge lower fees to clients who do not have insurance coverage than you routinely charge an insured client.
- Be sure clients know *they* are responsible for any charges that are not reimbursed by their insurance carriers, and bill clients regularly for any such charges. Be sure clients assign reimbursement to you if you are filing forms on their behalf.
- When payments are received, verify them against the claims submitted to be sure payment is in the correct amount. Refund any overpayments promptly, and request reconsideration of any underpayment.
- Review rejected claims promptly and prepare and submit written appeals for any processing errors. Request clarification for any rejected claim if the reason for rejection is not clear. Appeal that claim if you believe an error was made or if it was rejected because it was submitted by a professional counselor. (Contact the American Counseling Association for help in educating carriers.)
- Find out about claims and appeals procedures for any managed care, preferred provider organization, or health maintenance organization with which you may consider contracting.

Access to Facilities:
The Americans With Disabilities Act

Who Is Covered?

The Americans With Disabilities Act of 1990 (ADA) protects "qualified individuals with a disability" from discrimination on the basis of disability. People are considered disabled if they (1) have a physical or mental impairment that substantially limits one or more major life activity; (2) have a record of such an impairment; or (3) are regarded as having such an impairment. Specifically excluded from the definition of disability in the Act are homosexuality, bisexuality, transvestism, pedophilia, exhibitionism, voyeurism, gender identity disorders not resulting from physical impairments, or other sexual behavior disorders. Also excluded are compulsive gambling, kleptomania, pyromania, and psychoactive substance use disorders resulting from *current* illegal use of drugs (ADA, §511, 1990). Individuals who are currently using illegal drugs do not qualify for inclusion in programs offered by state and local government agencies either, with the exception of health and drug rehabilitation services.

People with disabilities must also be *qualified* to be protected by the ADA. In this case that means they *can meet the essential eligibility requirements to participate* in a program or receive services offered by a public entity with or without reasonable accommodations to rules, policies, or practices, the provision of auxiliary aids, or the removal of architectural, communication, or transportation barriers.

Public Accommodations

Title III of the ADA prohibits discrimination "on the basis of disability in the full and equal enjoyment of the goods, services, facilities, privileges, advantages, or accommodations of any place of public accommodation by any person who owns, leases (or leases to), or operates a place of public accommodation" (§302).

The ADA contains comprehensive definitions for most of these terms, but for our purposes it is important to know that privately owned and operated mental health counseling services, agencies, and practices are considered "public services." "Public Services" is one of the 12 categories of "public accommodations" that includes the offices of physicians, lawyers, or accountants, as well as businesses such as pharmacies, laundries, banks, and gas stations.

Public agencies operated by state and local governments are covered by Title II of the ADA and have separate affirmative obligations. Federal government agencies are covered by similar provisions of sections 501 and 504 of the Rehabilitation Act of 1973.

The U.S. Department of Justice is charged with enforcing this part of the ADA (the EEOC handles employment matters) and has published detailed regulations (28 C.F.R. §36). Paragraph 36.202 of those regulations generally

> provides that individuals with disabilities cannot be denied the opportunity to participate in or benefit from public accommodations; the opportunity offered disabled people must be equal to that offered non-disabled people; and the participation or benefit cannot be offered separately, unless that is the only effective way that a disabled person can participate in the program. (*ADA Compliance Guide*, 1990).

In practice, the Justice Department rules require the following:

- People with disabilities must be served by or admitted to public accommodations.
- A person cannot be denied the services or goods of an establishment because he or she has an association or relationship with a disabled person.
- If the policies, practices, or procedures of an establishment have the effect of excluding disabled people, *reasonable modifications* to those policies, practices, or procedures must be made unless they would fundamentally alter the nature of the business.
- *Auxiliary aids and services* must be provided to enable a person with a disability to use and enjoy the goods or services of an establishment, as long as the provision of the auxiliary aids does not pose an undue burden or is not disruptive to business.
- *Barriers* to accessibility in existing buildings must be removed if the removal is readily achievable.
- If a building is inaccessible to disabled people and removal of the barriers is not readily achievable, *alternative methods must be used to serve disabled people* if such methods would not impose an undue burden.
- Examinations and courses for professional or educational applications, testing, licensing, credentialing, or certification purposes must be accessible.
- *New buildings* must be constructed so they are accessible to and usable by disabled people.

- *When buildings are renovated,* the renovated areas and, under some circumstances, the path of travel and certain related facilities, must be accessible.[1]

All of these apply to counselors in private practice, and counselors must take affirmative steps to comply with the regulations to the extent they are not "unduly burdensome," "would not fundamentally alter the nature of the services provided," or, in the case of barrier removal, are "readily achievable" (easily accomplished without much difficulty or expense).

Some of these requirements are relatively easy to meet. Written materials produced on word processing programs can easily be reformatted to large text size to assist a client with vision problems. Some word processing programs can even produce materials in Brailled form through local service providers. Clearing furniture or potted plants that obstruct hallways, waiting rooms, and offices is a simple form of barrier removal. Installing ramps, grab bars, and raised toilets in restrooms, widening doorways, and creating designated parking spaces are all approaches recommended to address mobility impairments.

Many of the recommended measures are commonsense approaches to overcoming physical and mental limitations, but they are critically important to providing access to services for people with disabilities. It is important to *ask the person with a disability what auxiliary aids and services he or she needs* to benefit from your program. Not all blind people can read Braille. Not all people with hearing impairments can read lips or understand sign language. In fact, depending on the severity of the situation and the importance of the information to be communicated, a qualified sign language interpreter may be required. The counseling practice is probably required to pay for those services, since it is unlawful to charge people with disabilities for auxiliary aids and services or reasonable accommodations.

Individuals with disabilities can sue public accommodations for failing to comply with the provisions of the ADA, and the Justice Department is empowered to investigate complaints and litigate to

---

[1]Adapted with permission from *ADA Compliance Guide.* (1990–95). Washington, DC: Thompson Publishing Group. This is a two-volume loose-leaf service, with monthly updates, aimed at helping subscribers achieve compliance with the ADA. The book includes detailed explanations of the statute, regulations, technical materials, and diagrams, as well as practical advice for compliance. Subscription information is available by calling 1-800-677-3789.

compel compliance. At that stage, the courts may assess the full range of remedies, including damages, injunctive relief, "vindicating the public interest" through steep civil penalties, and awarding attorneys' fees. If you are not already familiar with your obligations under the ADA, it is important to formulate a plan for compliance now and to begin to implement it.

State and Local Government Entities

Title II of the ADA prohibits *all* state and local government entities from discriminating against *any* qualified individual with a disability in *any* program or activity they administer or operate. As in Title III, entities are required to provide reasonable accommodations, remove barriers, and provide auxiliary aids and services as required to permit full participation by individuals with disabilities, *unless* the agency can prove that "the action would result in a fundamental alteration in the nature of a service, program or activity or in undue financial and administrative burdens" (Nondiscrimination on Basis of Disability Rule, 1992).

There are a variety of administrative requirements for compliance with Title II, including conducting a self-evaluation of programs and practices. In addition, if the entity employs 50 or more people, the self-evaluation, and its resulting modifications, must remain open to inspection for 3 years. Entities also are required to inform the public of the rights afforded by the ADA and the entity's efforts to make programs accessible. Finally, entities with more than 50 employees also are required to appoint an ADA coordinator to serve as the agency's contact person on ADA compliance and to establish grievance procedures.

Licensure and Registration

As of March 1995, 41 states and the District of Columbia have statutes regulating the conduct and professional practice of mental health professionals (Morrissey, 1995). Whether through *registration, certification,* or *licensing statutes* (and the same terms vary somewhat in meaning from state to state) these states afford a measure of title protection for practicing professional counselors. Only those who have demonstrated their professional preparation and competency, usually by meeting minimum degree and experience requirements and passing an examination, may hold themselves out in the state as "licensed," "certified," or "registered" counselors.

There is some confusion among the states as to the differences between these titles. Anderson and Swanson (1994, pp. 23–24) distinguish them this way:

> A state occupational *license* affords protection of a professional title and scope of practice. . . . The effect of counselor licensure is the establishment of state control over a professional title and scope of professional activity. [emphasis in original]
>
> Governmental agencies grant *certification* to counselors who meet established criteria to engage in counseling practice. , . . Statutory certification is a privilege that authenticates counselor qualifications. It may also restrict the use of a professional title. [emphasis added]
>
> *Registration* . . . permits members of a profession to be registered with the state if they possess minimum credentials, thereby enabling them to practice their profession.

State licensure statutes also create licensing boards, determine the eligibility of those who may serve on the boards, and delineate their function. The primary purpose of such boards is to protect public health and safety by granting the privilege or license to individuals to engage in a professional practice under a professional title. Counselor licensing boards establish the minimum criteria for professional preparation and competence to enter into the counseling profession, regulate the conduct of professional counselors, and impose discipline on a professional counselor in the event of certain circumstances.

With state licensing may come certain privileges. First is protection of the professional title or designation. Only those who are duly licensed by their state licensing board may hold themselves out as licensed professional counselors, or however that title is designated in the licensing statute. In some states licensing gives professional counselors automatic inclusion as a licensed health provider, which may also result in inclusion in managed care programs and reimbursement for services. Anderson and Swanson (1994) point out that in Virginia, the first state to license counselors in 1976, counselors are also permitted to conduct testing services for schools, to use the terms *therapy* and *psychotherapy*, and are included in the privileged communication statute and in freedom-of-choice legislation for medical and mental health services.

Professional Liability Insurance

It should be evident by now that counselors can be prepared, competent, and licensed, learn about all the legal obligations and implications of counseling clients and operating a private business, scrupulously tailor their professional actions to conform to the *ACA Code of Ethics*, minimize all the potential risks they can control, and still become the target of ethical, administrative, or legal complaints. Clients may be dissatisfied with their progress in counseling, hear about a "hot" issue such as "repressed" memories of childhood sexual abuse on television or radio, or be encouraged by friends or relatives who have strong feelings about issues. They may have had unreasonable expectations about the results of counseling and blame the counselor when their lives do not improve. Consequently, even without any wrongdoing on the part of the counselor, an administrative or legal complaint may be filed against him or her. Some counselors do make mistakes that violate legal or ethical standards and escape penalty, but in today's litigious society it is unlikely that wrongdoing will go unreported. Most of these lawsuits stem from dual relationships with clients and sexual misconduct, not from mere mistakes in professional judgment.

A counselor must respond to any administrative, ethical, or legal complaint filed against him or her. Failure to respond to a complaint in court will automatically result in a default judgment against the defendant counselor, with damages ordered as the court determines appropriate. Even if the claim is found to be without merit at an early stage (before an actual trial), the costs to defend or negotiate that complaint may reach several thousand dollars. Legal expenses for a trial can exceed $50,000, and without insurance personal assets are at risk.

Counselors should include *professional liability insurance coverage* in their quality assurance plans just as comprehensive liability, employee benefits, and other coverage is routinely purchased for the professional practice. Average annual premium for professional liability coverage for counselors in 1995 was $350, well within the financial reach of most practicing professionals.

There are a number of factors to consider when purchasing professional liability coverage. Not all policies meet the needs of all counselors. Counselors may find coverage through individual policies, employee group plans, and plans sponsored by professional associations such as the ACA Insurance Trust. Policy coverage is usually of two types; for (1) *claims made* while the policy is in force and (2) for claims for alleged acts that occurred while the policy was in effect, even if the claim is made several years later after the policy is no longer in force (so-called *occurrence policies*). Because claims can be filed long after a client is no longer in counseling, the occurrence type of policy affords the greatest protection to the counselor. If your policy is of the claims-made type and you change to another insurance company, you will need to consider a separate policy that extends your coverage, usually called *tail coverage*.

It is important to secure coverage for all the aspects of your professional practice, including supervision of students or interns, consulting with other professionals, service on accreditation or professional review boards, and your work with clients. But be advised that most insurance contracts limit protection to situations where the conduct complained of was unintentional. Most professional liability policies *exclude* coverage for claims based on sexual misconduct and intentional wrongdoing such as fraud, dishonesty, or other criminal behavior. However, some policies will pay to defend the counselor in court against claims that are excluded, even though they will not pay damages if the counselor is held liable.

Even though they are not affiliated through a partnership or corporate entity, counselors sharing offices with other counselors are exposed to an increased risk of potential liability for the actions of the other counselors in the office. Liability insurance coverage for the entire group may be one way to minimize the risks for everyone in the group.

Paul L. Nelson (1995a), executive director of the ACA Insurance Trust, makes the following recommendations when shopping for insurance:

- Choose a carrier with a rating of "A" by an independent research company, such as A.M. Best, that signifies the company is on sound financial footing and has adequate reserve funds.
- Choose an insurance company that is an admitted (licensed) carrier so your state's Guaranty Fund will stand behind your carrier in the event of a default.
- Consider how long the company has been in the field of providing professional malpractice coverage and whether their rates have been stable.
- Does the company have a good record of service? How long does it take to get your policy and any needed endorsements? Are they accessible by telephone? Does the company provide a legal audit of your practice or help you in other ways to minimize or manage the risks associated with your practice?

Along with offering you the peace of mind that comes from knowing your insurance company will be by your side to defend you in the event of a lawsuit, some professional carriers will also help to minimize risks by providing training, publications, and other information for clients. Services such as the ACA Insurance Trust's Risk Management Hotline, where an attorney knowledgeable about the counseling profession can respond to potential malpractice questions, can help to avert lawsuits and administrative complaints before they are filed.

Reporting Unprofessional Conduct

Unpleasant as it may be, there will be times in any professional practice when issues arise that create suspicion that another practitioner is acting unprofessionally. According to the *ACA Code of Ethics*, when a professional counselor has "reasonable cause to believe that another counselor is violating an ethical standard," he or she has an ethical obligation to attempt to resolve the issue informally with the other counselor, provided "such action does not violate confidentiality rights" (H.2.d.). If informal resolution is not feasible, however, and only with *reasonable cause*, the counselor is to report "the suspected ethical violation to state or national ethics committees, unless this action conflicts with confidentiality rights that cannot be resolved" (H.2.e.).

In addition, many state licensing statutes require other licensed professionals to report unprofessional conduct to their state boards of professional review. Counselors are encouraged to determine the extent of their responsibilities in reporting such conduct in their states.

Responding to Ethical and Administrative Complaints

It is unlikely that you will ever receive a notice of an ethical or administrative complaint that you do not expect. Counselors usually are aware of a dispute with a client, relative of a client, or a colleague long before the complaint is filed. Even so, receiving the notice may still come as a surprise, and the resulting emotional concerns could cause even the most calm, competent professional to act in haste.

The first step once a notice is received should be to contact your professional liability carrier, if you have not done so prior to this time, to notify them of the charges. The second call should be to your attorney, or the attorney you are directed to by the insurer. Take the complaint seriously, and cooperate fully in the fact finding or investigation. Often, this will help to resolve the complaint at an informal level. Do not under any circumstances continue to treat a client who has filed a complaint against you or try to resolve the issue by "talking sense" to the client. Be sure to document your records, and consult with your attorney about the process of resolving the complaint, your conduct and how your actions relate to the standards by which you are being evaluated.

As the status of professional counselors has grown in the past 20 years, so has public scrutiny of their professional conduct. Counselors now are far more likely to be held up to external standards of preparation, competence, ethical values, and legal compliance, so it is imperative that you keep abreast of developments in the field and adjust your practice accordingly when changes are warranted. There is no question that you face a continuing challenge to apply legal and ethical standards to your practice, and it is likely that some situations simply will not fit within the established parameters. The risks are ongoing, but careful planning, thoughtful decision making, consultation with colleagues or legal advisers, and attention to the established ethical and legal standards can help you mitigate the risks and help you defend your actions if that ever becomes necessary.

SUGGESTED
READINGS

Herlihy, B., & Corey, G. (1992). *Dual relationships in counseling.* Alexandria, VA: American Counseling Association. Covers one of the most hotly debated topics facing the profession today. Fifteen respected professionals provide insight on handling difficult situations such as whether to accept a social invitation from a client, whether to refer a student to another advisor, or when and how to reveal information about your client or student.

Herlihy, B., & Corey, G. (1996). *ACA ethical standards casebook* (5th ed.), Alexandria, VA: American Counseling Association. Revised and updated to reflect changes in the *ACA Code of Ethics,* the casebook uses factual situations to discuss ethical choices and appropriate responses.

Huey, W. C. & Remley, T. P., Jr. (1989). *Ethical and legal issues in school counseling.* Alexandria, VA: American School Counselor Asscociation. Provides ethical and legal guidance on issues facing school counselors, such as confidentiality, privacy, privileged communication, access to school records, using ethical group techniques, computerized record keeping, and reporting unethical practices.

Remley, T. P., Jr. (Ed.). *ACA legal series.* Alexandria, VA: American Counseling Association. 1991–1994. This 12-volume series of monographs addresses single legal issues and includes guidelines for practice, answers to frequently asked questions, suggested readings, references, a glossary, and discussion questions.
>   Ahia, C. E., & Martin, D. (1993). The *Danger-to-self-or-others exception to confidentiality.*
>   Anderson. D., & Swanson, C. (1994). *Legal issues in licensure.*

Arthur, G. L., & Swanson, C. D. (1993). *Confidentiality and privileged communication.*

Bullis, R. K. (1992). *Law and management of a counseling agency or private practice.*

Crawford, R. L. (1994). *Avoiding counselor malpractice.*

Disney, M. J., & Stephens, A. M. (1994). *Legal issues in clinical supervision.*

Mitchell, R. W. (1991). *Documentation in counseling records.*

Remley, T. P., Jr. (1991). *Preparing for court appearances.*

Salo, M. M., & Shumate, S. G. (1993). *Counseling minor clients.*

Stevens-Smith, P., & Hughes, M. M. (1993). *Legal issues in marriage and family counseling.*

Strosnider, J. S., & Grad, J. D. (1993). *Third-party payments.*

Weikel, W. J., & Hughes, P. R. (1993). *The counselor as expert witness.*

REFERENCES

ADA Compliance Guide. (1990). Washington, DC: Thompson Publishing Group.

Age Discrimination in Employment Act of 1967, 29 U.S.C. §§621–634, as amended. (Implementing regulations found at 29 C.F.R. §1625.)

Ahia, C. E., & Martin, D. (1993). *The danger-to-self-or-others exception to confidentiality.* (*ACA Legal Series*, vol. 8). Alexandria, VA: American Counseling Association.

American Counseling Association. (1995). *ACA Code of ethics and standards of practice.* Alexandria, VA: Author.

American Medical Association. (1995). *Physicians Current Procedural Terminology (CPT).* Salt Lake City, UT: Medicode Publications.

American Psychiatric Association. (1994). *Diagnostic and Statistical Manual of Mental Disorders (DSM-IV).* Washington, DC: Author.

American Psychiatric Association. *Fact Sheet.* (1994). Washington, DC: Author.

Americans With Disabilities Act of 1990, 42 U.S.C.A. §12101 *et seq.*

Anderson, A. S. (1994). "When all else fails: Terminating the employment." *New challenges to the employer: Recent developments in employment law.* Seminar outline. Washington, DC: Educational Services Institute.

Anderson, D., & Swanson, C. D. (1994). *Legal issues in licensure* (*ACA Legal Series*, vol. 11). Alexandria, VA: American Counseling Association.

Arthur, G. L., Jr., & Swanson, C. D. (1993). *Confidentiality and privileged communication* (*ACA Legal Series*, vol. 6). Alexandria, VA: American Counseling Association.

Association for Specialists in Group Work (1989). *Ethical guidelines for group counselors.* Alexandria, VA: Author.

Bertram, B., & Wheeler, A. M. (1994). "Legal aspects of counseling: Avoiding lawsuits & legal problems." Workshop materials. Alexandria, VA: American Counseling Association.

Bogust v. Iverson, 10 Wis. 2d 129, 102 N.W.2d 228 (Wisc. 1960).

Boynton v. Burglass, 590 So. 2d 446 (Fla. Dist. Ct. App. 1991).

Bullis, R. K. (1993). *Law and management of a counseling agency or private practice (ACA Legal Series*, vol. 3). Alexandria, VA: American Counseling Association.

Camperlengo v. Barell, 585 N.E.2d 816 (N.Y. Ct. App. 1991).

Code of Virginia, §54.1–2400; §54.1–2914 (1994).

Coleman, F. T. (1995, January/February). Rethinking personnel strategies. *The Washington Lawyer, 9*(3), 39.

Corning Glass Works v. Brennan, 417 U.S. 188 (1974).

Crawford, Robert L. (1994). *Avoiding counselor malpractice (ACA Legal Series*, vol. 12). Alexandria, VA: American Counseling Association.

Criminal Law, 21 Am. Jur. 2d, §174.

Davis v. Lhim, 422 N.W.2d 688 (Mich. 1988).

Disney M. J., & Stephens, A. M. (1994). *Legal issues in clinical supervision (ACA Legal Series*, vol. 10). Alexandria, VA: American Counseling Association.

Doe v. Samaritan Counseling Center, 791 P.2d 344 (Alaska 1990).

Doe v. Wood, King County Super. Ct. (Wash.), No. 93-2-00985-2, Aug. 12, 1994.

Dunn & Bradstreet v. Robinson, 345 S.W.2d 34 (Ark. 1961).

Eisel v. Board of Education of Montgomery County, 324 Md. 376, 597 A.2d 447 (Md. Ct. App. 1991).

Equal Pay Act of 1963, 29 U.S.C. §206(d), as amended.

Family Educational Rights and Privacy Act, 20 U.S.C. §1232g (1974).

Family and Medical Leave Act of 1993, 29 U.S.C. §§2601 *et seq.*

Florida Rules of Criminal Procedure Re: Sentencing Guidelines, 576 So. 2d 1307 (Fla. Sup. Ct. 1991).

Garcia, J., Glosoff, H. L., & Smith, J. L. (1994). Report of the ACA Ethics Committee: 1993–1994. *Journal of Counseling & Development, 73*(2), 253–256.

Glosoff, H. L. (Dec. 1993). Be proactive when dealing with insurance companies. *Guidepost, 36*(6), 10.

Grote v. J.S. Mayer & Co., Inc., 570 N.E.2d 1146 (Ohio Ct. App. 1990).

Hamman v. County of Maricopa, 775 P.2d 1122, 161 Ariz. 58 (Ariz. Sup. Ct. 1989).

Hedlund v. Superior Court, 34 Cal. 3d 695, 669 P.2d 41 (1983).

Herlihy, B., & Corey, G. (1996). *ACA ethical standards casebook* (5th ed.). Alexandria, VA: American Counseling Association.

Herlihy, B., & Corey, G. (1992). *Dual relationships in counseling*. Alexandria, VA: American Counseling Association.

Hillman v. Columbia County, 474 N.W.2d 913 (Wis. Ct. App. 1991).

Hopkins, D. (October 1995). True therapy and false memory. *Counseling Today, 38*(4), 16.

Huey, E. C., & Remley, T. P., Jr. (Eds.). (1988). *Ethical and legal issues in school counseling*. Alexandria, VA: American Counseling Association.

Immigration Reform and Control Act of 1986, 8 U.S.C. §§1324a–1324b.

In re Doe, 964 F.2d 1325 (2d Cir. 1992).

In re Grand Jury Proceedings, 867 F.2d 562 (9th Cir.), *cert. denied*, 493 U.S. 906, 110 S. Ct. 265, 107 L. Ed. 2d 214 (1989).

In re Zuniga, 714 F.2d 632 (6th Cir.), *cert. denied*, 464 U.S. 983, 104 S. Ct. 426, 78 L. Ed. 2d 361 (1983).

Interest of L.L., 90 Wis. 2d 585, 280 N.W.2d 343 (Wis. App. 1979).

Jablonski v. United States, 712 F.2d 391 (9th Cir. 1983).

Jaffee v. Redmond, 51 F.3d 1346 (7th Cir. 1995), *cert. granted*, 116 S. Ct. 334, 64 U.S.L.W. 3143 (Oct. 16, 1995).

Johnston v. Rodis, 251 F.2d 917 (D.D.C. 1958). *See also* 99 A.L.R.2d 604, 605.

Kuehn v. Renton School Dist. No. 403, 694 P.2d 1078 (Wash. 1985).

Lovett, T. (1980, February). Exploring potential counselor liability in civil, criminal actions. *ASCA Newsletter*, pp. 3–4.

Mapp v. Ohio, 367 U.S. 643, 81 S. Ct. 1684, 6 L. Ed. 2d 1081 (1961).

Marino, T. W., (1995, February). Writing your way out of trouble. *Counseling Today*, 37(8), 8.

Minnesota v. Ohrtman, 466 N.W.2d 1 (Minn. Ct. App. 1991).

Missouri v. Beatty, 770 S.W.2d 387 (Mo. Ct. App. 1989).

Moesel, K.L., (Ed.), (1994, April), *Counselor Insurance News* (3)1, 4.

Morrissey, M. (Ed.). (1995, March). Persistence and patience named as keys to achieving licensure. *Counseling Today*, 37(9), 16.

Nally v. Grace Community Church, 204 Cal. Rptr. 303 (Cal. Ct. App. 1984); 253 Cal. Rptr. 97 (Cal. 1988), *rev'g* 240 Cal. Rptr. 215 (1987), *cert. denied*, 490 U.S. 1007, 109 S. Ct. 1644, 104 L. Ed. 2d 159 (1989).

Nelson, P. (1995b). *Report on inquiries and cases received by the ACA Insurance Trust, Inc.*

Nelson, P. (1995, July). Professional liability insurance—An important safety net. *Counseling Today*, 38(1), 19.

New Jersey v. T.L.O., 469 U.S. 325, 83 L. Ed. 2d 720, 105 S. Ct. 733 (1985).

Nondiscrimination on the Basis of Disability in State and Local Government Services Rule (1992), 28 C.F.R. §35.164.

Owens v. Scott Publishing Co., 284 P.2d 296 (Wash. 1955).

Peck v. Counseling Service of Addison County, Inc., 499 A.2d 422 (Vt. 1985).

Perriera v. Colorado, 768 P.2d 1198 (Colo. Sup. Ct. 1989).

Privacy Rights of Parents and Students, 34 C.F.R. §§99.1–99.37.

Regents of the University of Minnesota v. Applied Innovations, Inc., 876 F.2d 626 (8th Cir. 1989).

Remley, T. P., Jr. (1985). The law and ethical practices in elementary and middle schools. *Elementary School Guidance and Counseling*, 19(3), 181–189.

Remley, T. P., Jr. (1990). Counseling records: Legal and ethical issues. In Herlihy, B. & Golden, L. (Eds.), *ACA Ethical standards casebook* (pp. 162–169). Alexandria, VA: American Counseling Association.

Remley, T. P., Jr. (1993, May). Professional counselor identities. *ACA Guidepost, 35* (12), 4.

Robinson, S. E., & Gross, D. R. (1986). Ethics in mental health counseling. In A. J. Palmo & W. J. Weikel (Eds.), *Foundations of mental health counseling* (pp. 309–327). Springfield, IL: Charles C. Thomas.

Robinson, S. (1988). Counselor competence and malpractice suits: Opposite sides of the same coin. *Counseling and Human Development, 20*(9), 1–8.

Roe v. Wade, 410 U.S. 113 (1973).

Rosenberg v. Helinski, 616 A.2d 866 (Md. Ct. App. 1992).

Rust v. Sullivan, 500 U.S. 173 (1991).

Salo, M. M., & Shumate, S. G. (1993). *Counseling minor clients (ACA Legal Series*, vol. 4). Alexandria, VA: American Counseling Association.

Schuster v. Altenberg, 424 N.W.2d 159 (Wisc. 1988).

Searcy v. Auerbach, 980 F.2d 609 (9th Cir. 1992).

St. Paul Fire & Marine Ins. Co. v. Love, 459 N.W.2d 698 (Minn. Sup. Ct. 1990).

State v. Crary, 155 N.E.2d 262 (Ohio 1959).

State v. Woods, 307 N.C. 213, 297 S.E.2d 574 (1982).

Strosnider, J. S., & Grad, J. D. (1993). *Third-party payments* (ACA Legal Series, vol. 9). Alexandria, VA: American Counseling Association.

Suslovich v. New York Education Department, 571 N.Y.S.2d 123 (N.Y. App. Div. 1991).

Sutherland v. Kroger Co., 110 S.E.2d 716 (W.Va. 1959).

Tarasoff v. Regents of the University of California, 551 P.2d 334 (Cal. 1976).

Title VII of the Civil Rights Act of 1964, as amended by the Civil Rights Act of 1991, 42 U.S.C. §§2000e *et seq.* (Implementing regulations found at 29 C.F.R. §§1601–1613.)

United States v. Burtrum, 17 F.3d 1299 (10th Cir. 1994).

United States v. Corona, 849 F.2d 562 (11th Cir. 1988), *cert. denied,* 493 U.S. 906, 110 S. Ct. 265, 107 L. Ed. 2d 214 (1989).

United States v. Meagher, 531 F.2d 752 (5th Cir.), *cert. denied,* 429 U.S. 853, 97 S. Ct. 146, 50 L. Ed. 2d 128 (1976).

Vernonia School Dist. v. Acton, 1995 U.S. Lexis 4275 (1995).

Webster v. Reproductive Health Services, 492 U.S. 490, 109 S. Ct. 3040, 106 L. Ed. 2d 410 (1989).

Weikel, W. J., & Hughes, P. R. (1993). *The counselor as expert witness (ACA Legal Series,* vol. 5). Alexandria, VA: American Counseling Association.

World Health Organization. (1994). International Statistical Classification of Diseases and Related Health Problems (ICD-10). Albany, NY: Author.

Wigmore. (1961). *Evidence* §2332 (McNaughton Rev.).

Woman in false-memory case receives $2.6 million. (1995, Sept.). *Counseling Today*, *38*(3), 42.

Wozniak v. Lifoff, 242 Kan. 583, 750 P.2d 971 (1988).

ACA CODE OF ETHICS AND STANDARDS OF PRACTICE

Code of Ethics

Preamble

The American Counseling Association is an educational, scientific, and professional organization whose members are dedicated to the enhancement of human development throughout the life-span. Association members recognize diversity in our society and embrace a cross-cultural approach in support of the worth, dignity, potential, and uniqueness of each individual.

The specification of a code of ethics enables the association to clarify to current and future members, and to those served by members, the nature of the ethical responsibilities held in common by its members. As the code of ethics of the association, this document establishes principles that define the ethical behavior of association members. All members of the American Counseling Association are required to adhere to the Code of Ethics and the Standards of Practice. The Code of Ethics will serve as the basis for processing ethical complaints initiated against members of the association.

Section A: The Counseling Relationship

A.1. Client Welfare

a. *Primary Responsibility.* The primary responsibility of counselors is to respect the dignity and to promote the welfare of clients.

b. *Positive Growth and Development.* Counselors encourage client growth and development in ways that foster the clients' interest and welfare; counselors avoid fostering dependent counseling relationships.

c. *Counseling Plans*. Counselors and their clients work jointly in devising integrated, individual counseling plans that offer reasonable promise of success and are consistent with abilities and circumstances of clients. Counselors and clients regularly review counseling plans to ensure their continued viability and effectiveness, respecting clients' freedom of choice. (See A.3.b.)

d. *Family Involvement*. Counselors recognize that families are usually important in clients' lives and strive to enlist family understanding and involvement as a positive resource, when appropriate.

e. *Career and Employment Needs*. Counselors work with their clients in considering employment in jobs and circumstances that are consistent with the clients' overall abilities, vocational limitations, physical restrictions, general temperament, interest and aptitude patterns, social skills, education, general qualifications, and other relevant characteristics and needs. Counselors neither place nor participate in placing clients in positions that will result in damaging the interest and the welfare of clients, employers, or the public.

A.2. Respecting Diversity

a. *Nondiscrimination*. Counselors do not condone or engage in discrimination based on age, color, culture, disability, ethnic group, gender, race, religion, sexual orientation, marital status, or socioeconomic status. (See C.5.a., C.5.b., and D.1.i.)

b. *Respecting Differences*. Counselors will actively attempt to understand the diverse cultural backgrounds of the clients with whom they work. This includes, but is not limited to, learning how the counselor's own cultural/ethnic/racial identity impacts her or his values and beliefs about the counseling process. (See E.8. and F.2.i.)

A.3. Client Rights

a. *Disclosure to Clients*. When counseling is initiated, and throughout the counseling process as necessary, counselors inform clients of the purposes, goals, techniques, procedures, limitations, potential risks, and benefits of services to be performed, and other pertinent information. Counselors take steps to ensure that clients understand the implications of diagnosis, the intended use of tests and reports, fees, and billing arrangements. Clients have the right to expect confidentiality and to be provided with an explanation of its limitations, including supervision and/or treatment team professionals; to obtain clear information about their case records; to participate in the ongoing counseling plans; and to refuse any recommended services and be advised of the consequences of such refusal. (See E.5.a. and G.2.)

b. *Freedom of Choice.* Counselors offer clients the freedom to choose whether to enter into a counseling relationship and to determine which professional(s) will provide counseling. Restrictions that limit choices of clients are fully explained. (See A.1.c.)

c. *Inability to Give Consent.* When counseling minors or persons unable to give voluntary informed consent, counselors act in these clients' best interests. (See B.3.)

A.4. Clients Served by Others

If a client is receiving services from another mental health professional, counselors, with client consent, inform the professional persons already involved and develop clear agreements to avoid confusion and conflict for the client. (See C.6.c.)

A.5. Personal Needs and Values

a. *Personal Needs.* In the counseling relationship, counselors are aware of the intimacy and responsibilities inherent in the counseling relationship, maintain respect for clients, and avoid actions that seek to meet their personal needs at the expense of clients.

b. *Personal Values.* Counselors are aware of their own values, attitudes, beliefs, and behaviors and how these apply in a diverse society, and avoid imposing their values on clients. (See C.5.a.)

A.6. Dual Relationships

a. *Avoid When Possible.* Counselors are aware of their influen-tial positions with respect to clients, and they avoid exploiting the trust and dependency of clients. Counselors make every effort to avoid dual relationships with clients that could impair professional judgment or increase the risk of harm to clients. (Examples of such relationships include, but are not limited to, familial, social, financial, business, or close personal relationships with clients.) When a dual relationship cannot be avoided, counselors take appropriate professional precautions such as informed consent, consultation, supervision, and documentation to ensure that judgment is not impaired and no exploitation occurs. (See F.1.b.)

b. *Superior/Subordinate Relationships.* Counselors do not accept as clients superiors or subordinates with whom they have administrative, supervisory, or evaluative relationships.

A.7. Sexual Intimacies With Clients

a. *Current Clients.* Counselors do not have any type of sexual intimacies with clients and do not counsel persons with whom they have had a sexual relationship.

b. *Former Clients.* Counselors do not engage in sexual intimacies with former clients within a minimum of 2 years after terminating the counseling relationship. Counselors who engage in such relationship after 2 years following termination have the responsibility to examine and document thoroughly that such relations did not have an exploitative nature, based on factors such as duration of counseling, amount of time since counseling, termination circumstances, client's personal history and mental status, adverse impact on the client, and actions by the counselor suggesting a plan to initiate a sexual relationship with the client after termination.

A.8. Multiple Clients

When counselors agree to provide counseling services to two or more persons who have a relationship (such as husband and wife, or parents and children), counselors clarify at the outset which person or persons are clients and the nature of the relationships they will have with each involved person. If it becomes apparent that counselors may be called upon to perform potentially conflicting roles, they clarify, adjust, or withdraw from roles appropriately. (See B.2. and B.4.d.)

A.9. Group Work

a. *Screening.* Counselors screen prospective group counseling/therapy participants. To the extent possible, counselors select members whose needs and goals are compatible with goals of the group, who will not impede the group process, and whose well-being will not be jeopardized by the group experience.

b. *Protecting Clients.* In a group setting, counselors take reasonable precautions to protect clients from physical or psychological trauma.

A.10. Fees and Bartering
(See D.3.a. and D.3.b.)

a. *Advance Understanding.* Counselors clearly explain to clients, prior to entering the counseling relationship, all financial arrangements related to professional services including the use of collection agencies or legal measures for nonpayment. (A.11.c.)

b. *Establishing Fees.* In establishing fees for professional counseling services, counselors consider the financial status of clients and locality. In the event that the established fee structure is inappropriate for a client, assistance is provided in attempting to find comparable services of acceptable cost. (See A.10.d., D.3.a., and D.3.b.)

c. *Bartering Discouraged.* Counselors ordinarily refrain from accepting goods or services from clients in return for counseling services because such arrangements create inherent potential for conflicts, exploitation, and distortion of the professional relationship. Counselors may participate in bartering only if the relationship is not exploitative, if the client requests it, if a clear written contract is established, and if such arrangements are an accepted practice among professionals in the community. (See A.6.a.)

d. *Pro Bono Service.* Counselors contribute to society by devoting a portion of their professional activity to services for which there is little or no financial return (pro bono).

A.11. Termination and Referral

a. *Abandonment Prohibited.* Counselors do not abandon or neglect clients in counseling. Counselors assist in making appropriate arrangements for the continuation of treatment, when necessary, during interruptions such as vacations, and following termination.

b. *Inability to Assist Clients.* If counselors determine an inability to be of professional assistance to clients, they avoid entering or immediately terminate a counseling relationship. Counselors are knowledgeable about referral resources and suggest appropriate alternatives. If clients decline the suggested referral, counselors should discontinue the relationship.

c. *Appropriate Termination.* Counselors terminate a counseling relationship, securing client agreement when possible, when it is reasonably clear that the client is no longer benefiting, when services are no longer required, when counseling no longer serves the client's needs or interests, when clients do not pay fees charged, or when agency or institution limits do not allow provision of further counseling services. (See A.10.b. and C.2.g.)

A.12. Computer Technology

a. *Use of Computers.* When computer applications are used in counseling services, counselors ensure that (1) the client is intellectually, emotionally, and physically capable of using the computer application; (2) the computer application is appropriate for the needs of the client; (3) the client understands the purpose and operation of the computer applications; and (4) a follow-up of client use of a computer application is provided to correct possible misconceptions, discover inappropriate use, and assess subsequent needs.

b. *Explanation of Limitations.* Counselors ensure that clients are provided information as a part of the counseling relationship that adequately explains the limitations of computer technology.

c. *Access to Computer Applications.* Counselors provide for equal access to computer applications in counseling services. (See A.2.a.)

Section B: Confidentiality

B.1. Right to Privacy

a. *Respect for Privacy.* Counselors respect their clients' right to privacy and avoid illegal and unwarranted disclosures of confidential information. (See A.3.a. and B.6.a.)

b. *Client Waiver.* The right to privacy may be waived by the client or his or her legally recognized representative.

c. *Exceptions.* The general requirement that counselors keep information confidential does not apply when disclosure is required to prevent clear and imminent danger to the client or others or when legal requirements demand that confidential information be revealed. Counselors consult with other professionals when in doubt as to the validity of an exception.

d. *Contagious, Fatal Diseases.* A counselor who receives information confirming that a client has a disease commonly known to be both communicable and fatal is justified in disclosing information to an identifiable third party, who by his or her relationship with the client is at a high risk of contracting the disease. Prior to making a disclosure the counselor should ascertain that the client has not already informed the third party about his or her disease and that the client is not intending to inform the third party in the immediate future. (See B.1.c and B.1.f.)

e. *Court-Ordered Disclosure.* When court ordered to release confidential information without a client's permission, counselors request to the court that the disclosure not be required due to potential harm to the client or counseling relationship. (See B.1.c.)

f. *Minimal Disclosure.* When circumstances require the disclo-

sure of confidential information, only essential information is revealed. To the extent possible, clients are informed before confidential information is disclosed.

g. *Explanation of Limitations.* When counseling is initiated and throughout the counseling process as necessary, counselors inform clients of the limitations of confidentiality and identify foreseeable situations in which confidentiality must be breached. (See G.2.a.)

h. *Subordinates.* Counselors make every effort to ensure that privacy and confidentiality of clients are maintained by subordinates including employees, supervisees, clerical assistants, and volunteers. (See B.1.a.)

i. *Treatment Teams.* If client treatment will involve a continued review by a treatment team, the client will be informed of the team's existence and composition.

B.2. Groups and Families

a. *Group Work.* In group work, counselors clearly define confidentiality and the parameters for the specific group being entered, explain its importance, and discuss the difficulties related to confidentiality involved in group work. The fact that confidentiality cannot be guaranteed is clearly communicated to group members.

b. *Family Counseling.* In family counseling, information about one family member cannot be disclosed to another member without permission. Counselors protect the privacy rights of each family member. (See A.8., B.3., and B.4.d.)

B.3. Minor or Incompetent Clients

When counseling clients who are minors or individuals who are unable to give voluntary, informed consent, parents or guardians may be included in the counseling process as appropriate. Counselors act in the best interests of clients and take measures to safeguard confidentiality. (See A.3.c.)

B.4. Records

a. *Requirement of Records.* Counselors maintain records necessary for rendering professional services to their clients and as required by laws, regulations, or agency or institution procedures.

b. *Confidentiality of Records.* Counselors are responsible for securing the safety and confidentiality of any counseling records they create, maintain, transfer, or destroy whether the records are written, taped, computerized, or stored in any other medium. (See B.1.a.)

c. *Permission to Record or Observe.* Counselors obtain permission from clients prior to electronically recording or observing sessions. (See A.3.a.)

d. *Client Access.* Counselors recognize that counseling records are kept for the benefit of clients, and therefore provide access to records and copies of records when requested by competent clients, unless the records contain information that may be misleading and detrimental to the client. In situations involving multiple clients, access to records is limited to those parts of records that do not include confidential information related to another client. (See A.8., B.1.a., and B.2.b.)

e. *Disclosure or Transfer.* Counselors obtain written permission from clients to disclose or transfer records to legitimate third parties unless exceptions to confidentiality exist as listed in Section B.1. Steps are taken to ensure that receivers of counseling records are sensitive to their confidential nature.

B.5. Research and Training

a. *Data Disguise Required.* Use of data derived from counseling relationships for purposes of training, research, or publication is confined to content that is disguised to ensure the anonymity of the individuals involved. (See B.1.g. and G.3.d.)

b. *Agreement for Identification.* Identification of a client in a presentation or publication is permissible only when the client has reviewed the material and has agreed to its presentation or publication. (See G.3.d.)

B.6. Consultation

a. *Respect for Privacy.* Information obtained in a consulting relationship is discussed for professional

121

purposes only with persons clearly concerned with the case. Written and oral reports present data germane to the purposes of the consultation, and every effort is made to protect client identity and avoid undue invasion of privacy.

b. *Cooperating Agencies.* Before sharing information, counselors make efforts to ensure that there are defined policies in other agencies serving the counselor's clients that effectively protect the confidentiality of information.

Section C: Professional Responsibility

C.1. Standards Knowledge

Counselors have a responsibility to read, understand, and follow the Code of Ethics and the Standards of Practice.

C.2. Professional Competence

a. *Boundaries of Competence.* Counselors practice only within the boundaries of their competence, based on their education, training, supervised experience, state and national professional credentials, and appropriate professional experience. Counselors will demonstrate a commitment to gain knowledge, personal awareness, sensitivity, and skills pertinent to working with a diverse client population.

b. *New Specialty Areas of Practice.* Counselors practice in specialty areas new to them only after appropriate education, training, and supervised experience. While developing skills in new specialty areas, counselors take steps to ensure the competence of their work and to protect others from possible harm.

c. *Qualified for Employment.* Counselors accept employment only for positions for which they are qualified by education, training, supervised experience, state and national professional credentials, and appropriate professional experience. Counselors hire for professional counseling positions only individuals who are qualified and competent.

d. *Monitor Effectiveness.* Counselors continually monitor their effectiveness as professionals and take steps to improve when necessary. Counselors in private practice take reasonable steps to seek out peer supervision to evaluate their efficacy as counselors.

e. *Ethical Issues Consultation.* Counselors take reasonable steps to consult with other counselors or related professionals when they have questions regarding their ethical obligations or professional practice. (See H.1.)

f. *Continuing Education.* Counselors recognize the need for continuing education to maintain a reasonable level of awareness of current scientific and professional information in their fields of activity. They take steps to maintain competence in the skills they use, are open to new procedures, and keep current with the diverse and/or special populations with whom they work.

g. *Impairment*. Counselors refrain from offering or accepting professional services when their physical, mental, or emotional problems are likely to harm a client or others. They are alert to the signs of impairment, seek assistance for problems, and, if necessary, limit, suspend, or terminate their professional responsibilities. (See A.11.c.)

C.3. Advertising and Soliciting Clients

a. *Accurate Advertising*. There are no restrictions on advertising by counselors except those that can be specifically justified to protect the public from deceptive practices. Counselors advertise or represent their services to the public by identifying their credentials in an accurate manner that is not false, misleading, deceptive, or fraudulent. Counselors may only advertise the highest degree earned which is in counseling or a closely related field from a college or university that was accredited when the degree was awarded by one of the regional accrediting bodies recognized by the Council on Postsecondary Accreditation.

b. *Testimonials*. Counselors who use testimonials do not solicit them from clients or other persons who, because of their particular circumstances, may be vulnerable to undue influence.

c. *Statements by Others*. Counselors make reasonable efforts to ensure that statements made by others about them or the profession of counseling are accurate.

d. *Recruiting Through Employment*. Counselors do not use their places of employment or institutional affiliation to recruit or gain clients, supervisees, or consultees for their private practices. (See C.5.e.)

e. *Products and Training Advertisements*. Counselors who develop products related to their profession or conduct workshops or training events ensure that the advertisements concerning these products or events are accurate and disclose adequate information for consumers to make informed choices.

f. *Promoting to Those Served*. Counselors do not use counseling, teaching, training, or supervisory relationships to promote their products or training events in a manner that is deceptive or would exert undue influence on individuals who may be vulnerable. Counselors may adopt textbooks they have authored for instruction purposes.

g. *Professional Association Involvement*. Counselors actively participate in local, state, and national associations that foster the development and improvement of counseling.

C.4. Credentials

a. *Credentials Claimed*. Counselors claim or imply only professional credentials possessed and are responsible for correcting any known misrepresentations of their credentials by others. Professional credentials include graduate degrees in counseling or closely related mental health fields, accreditation of graduate programs, national voluntary certifications, government-issued certifications or licenses, ACA professional membership, or any other credential that might indicate to the public specialized knowledge or expertise in counseling.

b. *ACA Professional Membership.* ACA professional members may announce to the public their membership status. Regular members may not announce their ACA membership in a manner that might imply they are credentialed counselors.

c. *Credential Guidelines.* Counselors follow the guidelines for use of credentials that have been established by the entities that issue the credentials.

d. *Misrepresentation of Credentials.* Counselors do not attribute more to their credentials than the credentials represent, and do not imply that other counselors are not qualified because they do not possess certain credentials.

e. *Doctoral Degrees From Other Fields.* Counselors who hold a master's degree in counseling or a closely related mental health field, but hold a doctoral degree from other than counseling or a closely related field, do not use the title "Dr." in their practices and do not announce to the public in relation to their prac-

tice or status as a counselor that they hold a doctorate.

C.5. *Public Responsibility*

a. *Nondiscrimination.* Counselors do not discriminate against clients, students, or supervisees in a manner that has a negative impact based on their age, color, culture, disability, ethnic group, gender, race, religion, sexual orientation, or socioeconomic status, or for any other reason. (See A.2.a.)

b. *Sexual Harassment.* Counselors do not engage in sexual harassment. Sexual harassment is defined as sexual solicitation, physical advances, or verbal or nonverbal conduct that is sexual in nature, that occurs in connection with professional activities or roles, and that either (1) is unwelcome, is offensive, or creates a hostile workplace environment, and counselors know or are told this; or (2) is sufficiently severe or intense to be perceived as harassment to a reasonable person in the context. Sexual harassment can consist of a single intense or severe act or multiple persistent or pervasive acts.

c. *Reports to Third Parties.* Counselors are accurate, honest, and unbiased in reporting their professional activities and judgments to appropriate third parties including courts, health insurance companies, those who are the recipients of evaluation reports, and others. (See B.1.g.)

d. *Media Presentations.* When counselors provide advice or

comment by means of public lectures, demonstrations, radio or television programs, prerecorded tapes, printed articles, mailed material, or other media, they take reasonable precautions to ensure that (1) the statements are based on appropriate professional counseling literature and practice; (2) the statements are otherwise consistent with the Code of Ethics and the Standards of Practice; and (3) the recipients of the information are not encouraged to infer that a professional counseling relationship has been established. (See C.6.b.)

e. *Unjustified Gains.* Counselors do not use their professional positions to seek or receive unjustified personal gains, sexual favors, unfair advantage, or unearned goods or services. (See C.3.d.)

C.6. Responsibility to Other Professionals

a. *Different Approaches.* Counselors are respectful of approaches to professional counseling that differ from their own. Counselors know and take into account the traditions and practices of other professional groups with which they work.

b. *Personal Public Statements.* When making personal statements in a public context, counselors clarify that they are speaking from their personal perspectives and that they are not speaking on behalf of all counselors or the profession. (See C.5.d.)

c. *Clients Served by Others.* When counselors learn that their clients are in a professional relationship with another mental health professional, they request release from clients to inform the other professionals and strive to establish positive and collaborative professional relationships. (See A.4.)

Section D: Relationships With Other Professionals

D.1. Relationships With Employers and Employees

a. *Role Definition.* Counselors define and describe for their employers and employees the parameters and levels of their professional roles.

b. *Agreements.* Counselors establish working agreements with supervisors, colleagues, and subordinates regarding counseling or clinical relationships, confidentiality, adherence to professional standards, distinction between public and private material, maintenance and dissemination of recorded information, work load, and accountability. Working agreements in each instance are specified and made known to those concerned.

c. *Negative Conditions.* Counselors alert their employers to conditions that may be potentially disruptive or damaging to the counselor's professional responsibilities or that may limit their effectiveness.

d. *Evaluation.* Counselors submit regularly to professional review and evaluation by their supervisor or the appropriate representative of the employer.

e. *In-Service.* Counselors are responsible for in-service development of self and staff.

f. *Goals.* Counselors inform their staff of goals and programs.

g. *Practices.* Counselors provide personnel and agency practices that respect and enhance the rights and welfare of each employee and recipient of agency services. Counselors strive to maintain the highest levels of professional services.

h. *Personnel Selection and Assignment.* Counselors select competent staff and assign responsibilities compatible with their skills and experiences.

i. *Discrimination.* Counselors, as either employers or employees, do not engage in or condone practices that are inhumane, illegal, or unjustifiable (such as considerations based on age, color, culture, disability, ethnic group, gender, race, religion, sexual orientation, or socioeconomic status) in hiring, promotion, or training. (See A.2.a. and C.5.b.)

j. *Professional Conduct.* Counselors have a responsibility both to clients and to the agency or institution within which services are performed to maintain high standards of professional conduct.

k. *Exploitative Relationships.* Counselors do not engage in exploitative relationships with individuals over whom they have supervisory, evaluative, or instructional control or authority.

l. *Employer Policies.* The acceptance of employment in an agency or institution implies that counselors are in agreement with its general policies and principles. Counselors strive to reach agreement with employers as to acceptable standards of conduct that allow for changes in institutional policy conducive to the growth and development of clients.

D.2. Consultation (See B.6.)

a. *Consultation as an Option.* Counselors may choose to consult with any other professionally competent persons about their clients. In choosing consultants, counselors avoid placing the consultant in a conflict of interest situation that would preclude the consultant being a proper party to the counselor's efforts to help the client. Should counselors be engaged in a work setting that compromises this consultation standard, they consult with other professionals whenever possible to consider justifiable alternatives.

b. *Consultant Competency.* Counselors are reasonably certain that they have or the organization represented has the necessary competencies and resources for giving the kind of consulting services needed and that appropriate referral resources are available.

c. *Understanding With Clients.* When providing consultation, counselors attempt to develop with their clients a clear understanding of problem definition, goals for change, and predicted consequences of interventions selected.

d. *Consultant Goals.* The consulting relationship is one in which client adaptability and growth toward self-direction are consistently encouraged and cultivated. (See A.1.b.)

D.3. Fees for Referral

a. *Accepting Fees From Agency Clients.* Counselors refuse a private fee or other remuneration for rendering services to persons who are entitled to such services through the counselor's employing agency or institution. The policies of a particular agency may make explicit provisions for agency clients to receive counseling services from members of its staff in private practice. In such instances, the clients must be informed of other options open to them should they seek private counseling services. (See A.10.a., A.11.b., and C.3.d.)

b. *Referral Fees.* Counselors do not accept a referral fee from other professionals.

D.4. Subcontractor Arrangements

When counselors work as subcontractors for counseling services for a third party, they have a duty to inform clients of the limitations of confidentiality that the organiza-

tion may place on counselors in providing counseling services to clients. The limits of such confidentiality ordinarily are discussed as part of the intake session. (See B.1.e. and B.1.f.)

Section E: Evaluation, Assessment, and Interpretation

E.1. General

a. *Appraisal Techniques.* The primary purpose of educational and psychological assessment is to provide measures that are objective and interpretable in either comparative or absolute terms. Counselors recognize the need to interpret the statements in this section as applying to the whole range of appraisal techniques, including test and nontest data.

b. *Client Welfare.* Counselors promote the welfare and best interests of the client in the development, publication, and utilization of educational and psychological assessment techniques. They do not misuse assessment results and interpretations and take reasonable steps to prevent others from misusing the information these techniques provide. They respect the client's right to know the results, the interpretations made, and the bases for their conclusions and recommendations.

E.2. Competence to Use and Interpret Tests

a. *Limits of Competence.* Counselors recognize the limits of their competence and perform only those testing and assessment services for which they have been trained. They are familiar with reliability, validity, related standardization, error of measurement, and proper application of any technique utilized. Counselors using computer-based test interpretations are trained in the construct being measured and the specific instrument being used prior to using this type of computer application. Counselors take reasonable measures to ensure the proper use of psychological assessment techniques by persons under their supervision.

b. *Appropriate Use.* Counselors are responsible for the appropriate application, scoring, interpretation, and use of assessment instruments, whether they score and interpret such tests themselves or use computerized or other services.

c. *Decisions Based on Results.* Counselors responsible for decisions involving individuals or policies that are based on assessment results have a thorough understanding of educational and psychological measurement, including validation criteria, test research, and guidelines for test development and use.

d. *Accurate Information.* Counselors provide accurate information and avoid false claims or misconceptions when making statements about assessment instruments or techniques. Special efforts are made to avoid unwarranted connotations of such

terms as *IQ* and *grade equivalent scores.* (See C.5.c.)

E.3. Informed Consent

a. *Explanation to Clients.* Prior to assessment, counselors explain the nature and purposes of assessment and the specific use of results in language the client (or other legally authorized person on behalf of the client) can understand, unless an explicit exception to this right has been agreed upon in advance. Regardless of whether scoring and interpretation are completed by counselors, by assistants, or by computer or other outside services, counselors take reasonable steps to ensure that appropriate explanations are given to the client.

b. *Recipients of Results.* The examinee's welfare, explicit understanding, and prior agreement determine the recipients of test results. Counselors include accurate and appropriate interpretations with any release of individual or group test results. (See B.1.a. and C.5.c.)

E.4. Release of Information to Competent Professionals

a. *Misuse of Results.* Counselors do not misuse assessment results, including test results, and interpretations, and take reasonable steps to prevent the misuse of such by others. (See C.5.c.)

b. *Release of Raw Data.* Counselors ordinarily release data (e.g., protocols, counseling or interview notes, or questionnaires) in which the client is identified only with the consent of the client or the client's legal representative. Such data are usually released only to persons recognized by counselors as competent to interpret the data. (See B.1.a.)

E.5. Proper Diagnosis of Mental Disorders

a. *Proper Diagnosis.* Counselors take special care to provide proper diagnosis of mental disorders. Assessment techniques (including personal interview) used to determine client care (e.g., locus of treatment, type of treatment, or recommended follow-up) are carefully selected and appropriately used. (See A.3.a. and C.5.c.)

b. *Cultural Sensitivity.* Counselors recognize that culture affects the manner in which clients' problems are defined. Clients' socioeconomic and cultural experience is considered when diagnosing mental disorders.

E.6. Test Selection

a. *Appropriateness of Instruments.* Counselors carefully consider the validity, reliability, psychometric limitations, and appropriateness of instruments when selecting tests for use in a given situation or with a particular client.

b. *Culturally Diverse Populations.* Counselors are cautious when selecting tests for culturally diverse populations to avoid inappropriateness of testing that may be outside of socialized behavioral or cognitive patterns.

E.7. Conditions of Test Administration

a. *Administration Conditions.* Counselors administer tests under the same conditions that were established in their standardization. When tests are not administered under standard conditions or when unusual behavior or irregularities occur during the testing session, those conditions are noted in interpretation, and the results may be designated as invalid or of questionable validity.

b. *Computer Administration.* Counselors are responsible for ensuring that administration programs function properly to provide clients with accurate results when a computer or other electronic methods are used for test administration. (See A.12.b.)

c. *Unsupervised Test Taking.* Counselors do not permit unsupervised or inadequately supervised use of tests or assessments unless the tests or assessments are designed, intended, and validated for self-administration and/or scoring.

d. *Disclosure of Favorable Conditions.* Prior to test administration, conditions that produce most favorable test results are made known to the examinee.

E.8. Diversity in Testing

Counselors are cautious in using assessment techniques, making evaluations, and interpreting the performance of populations not represented in the norm group on which an instrument was standardized. They recognize the effects of age, color, culture, disability, ethnic group, gender, race, religion, sexual orientation, and socioeconomic status on test administration and interpretation and place test results in proper perspective with other relevant factors. (See A.2.a.)

E.9. Test Scoring and Interpretation

a. *Reporting Reservations.* In reporting assessment results, counselors indicate any reservations that exist regarding validity or reliability because of the circumstances of the assessment or the inappropriateness of the norms for the person tested.

b. *Research Instruments.* Counselors exercise caution when interpreting the results of research instruments possessing insufficient technical data to support respondent results. The specific purposes for the use of such instruments are stated explicitly to the examinee.

c. *Testing Services.* Counselors who provide test scoring and test interpretation services to support the assessment process confirm the validity of such interpretations. They accurately describe the purpose, norms, validity, reliability, and applications of the procedures and any special qualifications applicable to their use. The public offering of an automated test interpretations service is considered a professional-to-professional consultation. The formal responsibility of the consultant is to the consultee, but the ultimate and overriding responsibility is to the client.

E.10. Test Security

Counselors maintain the integrity and security of tests and other assessment techniques consistent with legal and contractual obligations. Counselors do not appropriate, reproduce, or modify published tests or parts thereof without acknowledgment and permission from the publisher.

E.11. Obsolete Tests and Outdated Test Results

Counselors do not use data or test results that are obsolete or outdated for the current purpose. Counselors make every effort to prevent the misuse of obsolete measures and test data by others.

E.12. Test Construction

Counselors use established scientific procedures, relevant standards, and current professional knowledge for test design in the development, publication, and utilization of educational and psychological assessment techniques.

Section F: Teaching, Training, and Supervision

F.1. Counselor Educators and Trainers

a. *Educators as Teachers and Practitioners.* Counselors who are responsible for developing, implementing, and supervising educational programs are skilled as teachers and practitioners. They are knowledgeable regarding the ethical, legal, and regulatory aspects of the profession, are skilled in applying that knowledge, and make students and supervisees aware of their responsibilities. Counselors conduct counselor education and training programs in an ethical manner and serve as role models for professional behavior. Counselor educators should make an effort to infuse material related to human diversity into all courses and/or workshops that are designed to promote the development of professional counselors.

b. *Relationship Boundaries With Students and Supervisees*. Counselors clearly define and maintain ethical, professional, and social relationship boundaries with their students and supervisees. They are aware of the differential in power that exists and the student's or supervisee's possible incomprehension of that power differential. Counselors explain to students and supervisees the potential for the relationship to become exploitive.

c. *Sexual Relationships*. Counselors do not engage in sexual relationships with students or supervisees and do not subject them to sexual harassment. (See A.6. and C.5.b)

d. *Contributions to Research*. Counselors give credit to students or supervisees for their contributions to research and scholarly projects. Credit is given through coauthorship, acknowledgment, footnote statement, or other appropriate means, in accordance with such contributions. (See G.4.b. and G.4.c.)

e. *Close Relatives*. Counselors do not accept close relatives as students or supervisees.

f. *Supervision Preparation*. Counselors who offer clinical supervision services are adequately prepared in supervision methods and techniques. Counselors who are doctoral students serving as practicum or internship supervisors to master's level students are adequately prepared and supervised by the training program.

g. *Responsibility for Services to Clients*. Counselors who supervise the counseling services of others take reasonable measures to ensure that counseling services provided to clients are professional.

h. *Endorsement*. Counselors do not endorse students or supervisees for certification, licensure, employment, or completion of an academic or training program if they believe students or supervisees are not qualified for the endorsement. Counselors take reasonable steps to assist students or supervisees who are not qualified for endorsement to become qualified.

F.2. Counselor Education and Training Programs

a. *Orientation*. Prior to admission, counselors orient prospective students to the counselor education or training program's expectations, including but not limited to the following: (1) the type and level of skill acquisition required for successful completion of the training, (2) subject matter to be covered, (3) basis for evaluation, (4) training components that encourage self-growth or self-disclosure as part of the training process, (5) the type of supervision settings and requirements of the sites for required clinical field experiences, (6) student and supervisee evaluation and dismissal policies and procedures, and (7) up-to-date employment prospects for graduates.

b. *Integration of Study and Practice.* Counselors establish counselor education and training programs that integrate academic study and supervised practice.

c. *Evaluation.* Counselors clearly state to students and supervisees, in advance of training, the levels of competency expected, appraisal methods, and timing of evaluations for both didactic and experiential components. Counselors provide students and supervisees with periodic performance appraisal and evaluation feedback throughout the training program.

d. *Teaching Ethics.* Counselors make students and supervisees aware of the ethical responsibilities and standards of the profession and the students' and supervisees' ethical responsibilities to the profession. (See C.1. and F.3.e.)

e. *Peer Relationships.* When students or supervisees are assigned to lead counseling groups or provide clinical supervision for their peers, counselors take steps to ensure that students and supervisees placed in these roles do not have personal or adverse relationships with peers and that they understand they have the same ethical obligations as counselor educators, trainers, and supervisors. Counselors make every effort to ensure that the rights of peers are not compromised when students or supervisees are assigned to lead counseling groups or provide clinical supervision.

f. *Varied Theoretical Positions.* Counselors present varied theoretical positions so that students and supervisees may make comparisons and have opportunities to develop their own positions. Counselors provide information concerning the scientific bases of professional practice. (See C.6.a.)

g. *Field Placements.* Counselors develop clear policies within their training program regarding field placement and other clinical experiences. Counselors provide clearly stated roles and responsibilities for the student or supervisee, the site supervisor, and the program supervisor. They confirm that site supervisors are qualified to provide supervision and are informed of their professional and ethical responsibilities in this role.

h. *Dual Relationships as Supervisors.* Counselors avoid dual relationships such as performing the role of site supervisor and training program supervisor in the student's or supervisee's training program. Counselors do not accept any form of professional services, fees, commissions, reimbursement, or remuneration from a site for student or supervisee placement.

i. *Diversity in Programs.* Counselors are responsive to their institution's and program's recruitment and retention needs for training program administrators, faculty, and students with diverse backgrounds and special needs. (See A.2.a.)

F.3. Students and Supervisees

a. *Limitations.* Counselors, through ongoing evaluation and appraisal, are aware of the academic and personal limitations of students and supervisees that might impede performance. Counselors assist students and supervisees in securing remedial assistance when needed, and dismiss from the training program supervisees who are unable to provide competent service due to academic or personal limitations. Counselors seek professional consultation and document their decision to dismiss or refer students or supervisees for assistance. Counselors ensure that students and supervisees have recourse to address decisions made to require them to seek assistance or to dismiss them.

b. *Self-Growth Experiences.* Counselors use professional judgment when designing training experiences conducted by the counselors themselves that require student and supervisee self-growth or self-disclosure. Safeguards are provided so that students and supervisees are aware of the ramifications their self-disclosure may have on counselors whose primary role as teacher, trainer, or supervisor requires acting on ethical obligations to the profession. Evaluative components of experiential training experiences explicitly delineate predetermined academic standards that are separate and do not dependent on the student's level of self-disclosure. (See A.6.)

c. *Counseling for Students and Supervisees.* If students or supervisees request counseling, supervisors or counselor educators provide them with acceptable referrals. Supervisors or counselor educators do not serve as counselor to students or supervisees over whom they hold administrative, teaching, or evaluative roles unless this is a brief role associated with a training experience. (See A.6.b.)

d. *Clients of Students and Supervisees.* Counselors make every effort to ensure that the clients at field placements are aware of the services rendered and the qualifications of the students and supervisees rendering those services. Clients receive professional disclosure information and are informed of the limits of confidentiality. Client permission is obtained in order for the students and supervisees to use any information concerning the counseling relationship in the training process. (See B.1.e.)

e. *Standards for Students and Supervisees*. Students and supervisees preparing to become counselors adhere to the Code of Ethics and the Standards of Practice. Students and supervisees have the same obligations to clients as those required of counselors. (See H.1.)

Section G: Research and Publication

G.1. Research Responsibilities

a. *Use of Human Subjects*. Counselors plan, design, conduct, and report research in a manner consistent with pertinent ethical principles, federal and state laws, host institutional regulations, and scientific standards governing research with human subjects. Counselors design and conduct research that reflects cultural sensitivity appropriateness.

b. *Deviation From Standard Practices*. Counselors seek consultation and observe stringent safeguards to protect the rights of research participants when a research problem suggests a deviation from standard acceptable practices. (See B.6.)

c. *Precautions to Avoid Injury*. Counselors who conduct research with human subjects are responsible for the subjects' welfare throughout the experiment and take reasonable precautions to avoid causing injurious psychological, physical, or social effects to their subjects.

d. *Principal Researcher Responsibility*. The ultimate responsibility for ethical research practice lies with the principal researcher. All others involved in the research activities share ethical obligations and full responsibility for their own actions.

e. *Minimal Interference*. Counselors take reasonable precautions to avoid causing disruptions in subjects' lives due to participation in research.

f. *Diversity*. Counselors are sensitive to diversity and research issues with special populations. They seek consultation when appropriate. (See A.2.a. and B.6.)

G.2. Informed Consent

a. *Topics Disclosed*. In obtaining informed consent for research, counselors use language that is understandable to research participants and that (1) accurately explains the purpose and procedures to be followed; (2) identifies any procedures that are experimental or relatively untried; (3) describes the attendant discomforts and risks; (4) describes the benefits or changes in individuals or organizations that might be reasonably expected; (5) discloses appropriate alternative procedures that would be advantageous for subjects; (6) offers to answer any inquiries concerning the procedures; (7) describes any limitations on confidentiality; and (8) instructs that subjects are free to withdraw their consent and to discontinue participation in the project at any time. (See B.1.f.)

b. *Deception.* Counselors do not conduct research involving deception unless alternative procedures are not feasible and the prospective value of the research justifies the deception. When the methodological requirements of a study necessitate concealment or deception, the investigator is required to explain clearly the reasons for this action as soon as possible.

c. *Voluntary Participation.* Participation in research is typically voluntary and without any penalty for refusal to participate. Involuntary participation is appropriate only when it can be demonstrated that participation will have no harmful effects on subjects and is essential to the investigation.

d. *Confidentiality of Information.* Information obtained about research participants during the course of an investigation is confidential. When the possibility exists that others may obtain access to such information, ethical research practice requires that the possibility, together with

the plans for protecting confidentiality, be explained to participants as a part of the procedure for obtaining informed consent. (See B.1.e.)

e. *Persons Incapable of Giving Informed Consent.* When a person is incapable of giving informed consent, counselors provide an appropriate explanation, obtain agreement for participation, and obtain appropriate consent from a legally authorized person.

f. *Commitments to Participants.* Counselors take reasonable measures to honor all commitments to research participants.

g. *Explanations After Data Collection.* After data are collected, counselors provide participants with full clarification of the nature of the study to remove any misconceptions. Where scientific or human values justify delaying or withholding information, counselors take reasonable measures to avoid causing harm.

h. *Agreements to Cooperate.* Counselors who agree to cooperate with another individual in research or publication incur an obligation to cooperate as promised in terms of punctuality of performance and with regard to the completeness and accuracy of the information required.

i. *Informed Consent for Sponsors.* In the pursuit of research, counselors give sponsors, institutions, and publication channels the same respect and opportunity for giving informed consent that they accord to individual research participants. Counselors are aware of their obligation to future research workers and ensure that host institutions are given feedback information and proper acknowledgment.

G.3. Reporting Results

a. *Information Affecting Outcome.* When reporting research results, counselors explicitly mention all variables and conditions known to the investigator that may have affected the outcome of a study or the interpretation of data.

b. *Accurate Results.* Counselors plan, conduct, and report research accurately and in a manner that minimizes the possibility that results will be misleading. They provide thorough discussions of the limitations of their data and alternative hypotheses. Counselors do not engage in fraudulent research, distort data, misrepresent data, or deliberately bias their results.

c. *Obligation to Report Unfavorable Results.* Counselors communicate to other counselors the results of any research judged to be of professional value. Results that reflect unfavorably on institutions, programs, services, prevailing opinions, or vested interests are not withheld.

d. *Identity of Subjects.* Counselors who supply data, aid in the research of another person, report research results, or make original data available take due care to disguise the identity of respective subjects in the absence of specific authorization from the

subjects to do otherwise. (See B.1.g. and B.5.a.)

e. *Replication Studies.* Counselors are obligated to make available sufficient original research data to qualified professionals who may wish to replicate the study.

G.4. Publication

a. *Recognition of Others.* When conducting and reporting research, counselors are familiar with and give recognition to previous work on the topic, observe copyright laws, and give full credit to those to whom credit is due. (See F.1.d. and G.4.c.)

b. *Contributors.* Counselors give credit through joint authorship, acknowledgment, footnote statements, or other appropriate means to those who have contributed significantly to research or concept development in accordance with such contributions. The principal contributor is listed first and minor technical or professional contributions are acknowledged in notes or introductory statements.

c. *Student Research.* For an article that is substantially based on a student's dissertation or thesis, the student is listed as the principal author. (See F.1.d. and G.4.a.)

d. *Duplicate Submission.* Counselors submit manuscripts for consideration to only one journal at a time. Manuscripts that are published in whole or in substantial part in another journal or published work are not submitted for publication without acknowledgment and permission from the previous publication.

e. *Professional Review.* Counselors who review material submitted for publication, research, or other scholarly purposes respect the confidentiality and proprietary rights of those who submitted it.

Section H:
Resolving Ethical Issues

H.1. Knowledge of Standards

Counselors are familiar with the Code of Ethics and the Standards of Practice and other applicable ethics codes from other professional organizations of which they are member, or from certification and licensure bodies. Lack of knowledge or misunderstanding of an ethical responsibility is not a defense against a charge of unethical conduct. (See F.3.e.)

H.2. Suspected Violations

a. *Ethical Behavior Expected.* Counselors expect professional associates to adhere to the Code of Ethics. When counselors possess reasonable cause that raises doubts as to whether a counselor is acting in an ethical manner, they take appropriate action. (See H.2.d. and H.2.e.)

b. *Consultation.* When uncertain as to whether a particular situation or course of action may be in violation of the Code of Ethics, counselors consult with other counselors who are knowledgeable about ethics, with colleagues, or with appropriate authorities.

c. *Organization Conflicts.* If the demands of an organization with which counselors are affiliated pose a conflict with the Code of Ethics, counselors specify the nature of such conflicts and express to their supervisors or other responsible officials their commitment to the Code of Ethics. When possible, counselors work toward change within the organization to allow full adherence to the Code of Ethics.

d. *Informal Resolution.* When counselors have reasonable cause to believe that another counselor is violating an ethical standard, they attempt to first resolve the issue informally with the other counselor if feasible, providing that such action does not violate confidentiality rights that may be involved.

e. *Reporting Suspected Violations.* When an informal resolution is not appropriate or feasible, counselors, upon reasonable cause, take action such as reporting the suspected ethical violation to state or national ethics committees, unless this action conflicts with confidentiality rights that cannot be resolved.

f. *Unwarranted Complaints.* Counselors do not initiate, participate in, or encourage the filing of ethics complaints that are unwarranted or intend to harm a counselor rather than to protect clients or the public.

137

H.3. Cooperation With Ethics Committees

Counselors assist in the process of enforcing the Code of Ethics. Counselors cooperate with investigations, proceedings, and requirements of the ACA Ethics Committee or ethics committees of other duly constituted associations or boards having jurisdiction over those charged with a violation. Counselors are familiar with the ACA Policies and Procedures and use it as a reference in assisting the enforcement of the Code of Ethics.

Standards of Practice

All members of the American Counseling Association (ACA) are required to adhere to the Standards of Practice and the Code of Ethics. The Standards of Practice represent minimal behavioral statements of the Code of Ethics. Members should refer to the applicable section of the Code of Ethics for further interpretation and amplification of the applicable Standard of Practice.

Section A:
The Counseling Relationship

Standard of Practice One (SP-1): Nondiscrimination. Counselors respect diversity and must not discriminate against clients because of age, color, culture, disability, ethnic group, gender, race, religion, sexual orientation, marital status, or socioeconomic status. (See A.2.a.)

Standard of Practice Two (SP-2): Disclosure to Clients. Counselors must adequately inform clients, preferably in writing, regarding the counseling process and counseling relationship at or before the time it begins and throughout the relationship. (See A.3.a.)

Standard of Practice Three (SP-3): Dual Relationships. Counselors must make every effort to avoid dual relationships with clients that could impair their professional judgment or increase the risk of harm to clients. When a dual relationship cannot be avoided, counselors must take appropriate steps to ensure that judgment is not impaired and that no exploitation occurs. (See A.6.a. and A.6.b.)

Standard of Practice Four (SP-4): Sexual Intimacies With Clients. Counselors must not engage in any type of sexual intimacies with current clients and must not engage in sexual intimacies with former clients within a minimum of 2 years after terminating the counseling relationship. Counselors who engage in such relationship after 2 years following termination have the responsibility to examine and document thoroughly that such relations did not have an exploitative nature.

138

Standard of Practice Five (SP-5): Protecting Clients During Group Work. Counselors must take steps to protect clients from physical or psychological trauma resulting from interactions during group work. (See A.9.b.)

Standard of Practice Six (SP-6): Advance Understanding of Fees. Counselors must explain to clients, prior to their entering the counseling relationship, financial arrangements related to professional services. (See A.10. a.-d. and A.11.c.)

Standard of Practice Seven (SP-7): Termination. Counselors must assist in making appropriate arrangements for the continuation of treatment of clients, when necessary, following termination of counseling relationships. (See A.11.a.)

Standard of Practice Eight (SP-8): Inability to Assist Clients. Counselors must avoid entering or immediately terminate a counseling relationship if it is determined that they are unable to be of professional assistance to a client. The counselor may assist in making an appropriate referral for the client. (See A.11.b.)

Section B: Confidentiality

Standard of Practice Nine (SP-9): Confidentiality Requirement. Counselors must keep information related to counseling services confidential unless disclosure is in the best interest of clients, is required for the welfare of others, or is required by law. When disclosure is required, only information that is essential is revealed and the client is informed of such disclosure. (See B.1. a.-f.)

Standard of Practice Ten (SP-10): Confidentiality Requirements for Subordinates. Counselors must take measures to ensure that privacy and confidentiality of clients are maintained by subordinates. (See B.1.h.)

Standard of Practice Eleven (SP-11): Confidentiality in Group Work. Counselors must clearly communicate to group members that confidentiality cannot be guaranteed in group work. (See B.2.a.)

Standard of Practice Twelve (SP-12): Confidentiality in Family Counseling . Counselors must not disclose information about one family member in counseling to another family member without prior consent. (See B.2.b.)

Standard of Practice Thirteen (SP-13): Confidentiality of Records. Counselors must maintain appropriate confidentiality in creating, storing, accessing, transferring, and disposing of counseling records. (See B.4.b.)

Standard of Practice Fourteen (SP-14): Permission to Record or Observe. Counselors must obtain prior consent from clients in order to record electronically or observe sessions. (See B.4.c.)

Standard of Practice Fifteen (SP-15): Disclosure or Transfer of Records. Counselors must obtain client consent to disclose or transfer records to third parties, unless exceptions listed in SP-9 exist. (See B.4.e.)

Standard of Practice Sixteen (SP-16): Data Disguise Required. Counselors must disguise the identity of the client when using data for training, research, or publication. (See B.5.a.)

Section C: Professional Responsibility

Standard of Practice Seventeen (SP-17): Boundaries of Competence. Counselors must practice only within the boundaries of their competence. (See C.2.a.)

Standard of Practice Eighteen (SP-18): Continuing Education. Counselors must engage in continuing education to maintain their professional competence. (See C.2.f.)

Standard of Practice Nineteen (SP-19): Impairment of Professionals. Counselors must refrain from offering professional services when their personal problems or conflicts may cause harm to a client or others. (See C.2.g.)

Standard of Practice Twenty (SP-20): Accurate Advertising. Counselors must accurately represent their credentials and services when advertising. (See C.3.a.)

Standard of Practice Twenty-One (SP-21): Recruiting Through Em-ployment. Counselors must not use their place of employment or institutional affiliation to recruit clients for their private practices. (See C.3.d.)

Standard of Practice Twenty-Two (SP-22): Credentials Claimed. Counselors must claim or imply only professional credentials possessed and must correct any known misrepresentations of their credentials by others. (See C.4.a.)

Standard of Practice Twenty-Three (SP-23): Sexual Harassment. Counselors must not engage in sexual harassment. (See C.5.b.)

Standard of Practice Twenty-Four (SP-24): Unjustified Gains. Counselors must not use their professional positions to seek or receive unjustified personal gains, sexual favors, unfair advantage, or unearned goods or services. (See C.5.e.)

Standard of Practice Twenty-Five (SP-25): Clients Served by Others. With the consent of the client, counselors must inform other mental health professionals serving the same client that a counseling relationship between the counselor and client exists. (See C.6.c.)

Standard of Practice Twenty-Six (SP-26): Negative Employment Conditions. Counselors must alert their employers to institutional policy or conditions that may be potentially disruptive or damaging to the counselor's professional responsibilities, or that may limit their effectiveness or deny clients' rights. (See D.1.c.)

Standard of Practice Twenty-Seven (SP-27): Personnel Selection and Assignment. Counselors must select competent staff and must assign responsibilities compatible with staff skills and experiences. (See D.1.h.)

Standard of Practice Twenty-Eight (SP-28): Exploitative Relationships With Subordinates. Counselors must not engage in exploitative relationships with individuals over whom they have supervisory, evaluative, or instructional control or authority. (See D.1.k.)

Section D: Relationship With Other Professionals

Standard of Practice Twenty-Nine (SP-29): Accepting Fees From Agency Clients. Counselors must not accept fees or other remuneration for consultation with persons entitled to such services through the counselor's employing agency or institution. (See D.3.a.)

Standard of Practice Thirty (SP-30): Referral Fees. Counselors must not accept referral fees. (See D.3.b.)

Section E: Evaluation, Assessment, and Interpretation

Standard of Practice Thirty-One (SP-31): Limits of Competence. Counselors must perform only testing and assessment services for which they are competent. Counselors must not allow the use of

psychological assessment techniques by unqualified persons under their supervision. (See E.2.a.)

Standard of Practice Thirty-Two (SP-32): Appropriate Use of Assessment Instruments. Counselors must use assessment instruments in the manner for which they were intended. (See E.2.b.)

Standard of Practice Thirty-Three (SP-33): Assessment Explanations to Clients. Counselors must provide explanations to clients prior to assessment about the nature and purposes of assessment and the specific uses of results. (See E.3.a.)

Standard of Practice Thirty-Four (SP-34): Recipients of Test Results. Counselors must ensure that accurate and appropriate interpretations accompany any release of testing and assessment information. (See E.3.b.)

Standard of Practice Thirty-Five (SP-35): Obsolete Tests and Outdated Test Results. Counselors must not base their assessment or intervention decisions or recommendations on data or test results that are obsolete or outdated for the current purpose. (See E.11.)

Section F: Teaching, Training, and Supervision

Standard of Practice Thirty-Six (SP-36): Sexual Relationships With Students or Supervisees. Counselors must not engage in sexual relationships with their students and supervisees. (See F.1.c.)

141

Standard of Practice Thirty-Seven (SP-37): Credit for Contributions to Research. Counselors must give credit to students or supervisees for their contributions to research and scholarly projects. (See F.1.d.)

Standard of Practice Thirty-Eight (SP-38): Supervision Preparation. Counselors who offer clinical supervision services must be trained and prepared in supervision methods and techniques. (See F.1.f.)

Standard of Practice Thirty-Nine (SP-39): Evaluation Information. Counselors must clearly state to students and supervisees in advance of training the levels of competency expected, appraisal methods, and timing of evaluations. Counselors must provide students and supervisees with periodic performance appraisal and evaluation feedback throughout the training program. (See F.2.c.)

Standard of Practice Forty (SP-40): Peer Relationships in Training. Counselors must make every effort to ensure that the rights of peers are not violated when students and supervisees are assigned to lead counseling groups or provide clinical supervision. (See F.2.e.)

Standard of Practice Forty-One (SP-41): Limitations of Students and Supervisees. Counselors must assist students and supervisees in securing remedial assistance, when needed, and must dismiss from the training program students and supervisees who are unable to provide competent service due to academic or personal limitations. (See F.3.a.)

Standard of Practice Forty-Two (SP-42): Self-Growth Experiences. Counselors who conduct experiences for students or supervisees that include self-growth or self-disclosure must inform participants of counselors' ethical obligations to the profession and must not grade participants based on their nonacademic performance. (See F.3.b.)

Standard of Practice Forty-Three (SP-43): Standards for Students and Supervisees. Students and supervisees preparing to become counselors must adhere to the Code of Ethics and the Standards of Practice of counselors. (See F.3.e.)

Section G: Research and Publication

Standard of Practice Forty-Four (SP-44): Precautions to Avoid Injury in Research. Counselors must avoid causing physical, social, or psychological harm or injury to subjects in research. (See G.1.c.)

Standard of Practice Forty-Five (SP-45): Confidentiality of Research Information. Counselors must keep confidential information obtained about research participants. (See G.2.d.)

Standard of Practice Forty-Six (SP-46): Information Affecting Research Outcome. Counselors must report all variables and conditions known to the investigator that may have affected research data or outcomes. (See G.3.a.)

Standard of Practice Forty-Seven (SP-47): Accurate Research Results. Counselors must not distort or misrepresent research data, nor fabricate or intentionally bias research results. (See G.3.b.)

Standard of Practice Forty-Eight (SP-48): Publication Contributors. Counselors must give appropriate credit to those who have contributed to research. (See G.4.a. and G.4.b.)

Section H: Resolving Ethical Issues

Standard of Practice Forty-Nine (SP-49): Ethical Behavior Expected. Counselors must take appropriate action when they possess reasonable cause that raises doubts as to whether counselors or other mental health professionals are acting in an ethical manner. (See H.2.a.)

Standard of Practice Fifty (SP-50): Unwarranted Complaints. Counselors must not initiate, participate in, or encourage the filing of ethics complaints that are unwarranted or intended to harm a mental health professional rather than to protect clients or the public. (See H.2.f.)

Standard of Practice Fifty-One (SP-51): Cooperation With Ethics Committees. Counselors must cooperate with investigations, proceedings, and requirements of the ACA Ethics Committee or ethics committees of other duly constituted associations or boards having jurisdiction over those charged with a violation. (See H.3.)

References

The following documents are available to counselors as resources to guide them in their practices. These resources are not a part of the Code of Ethics and the Standards of Practice.

American Association for Counseling and Development/Association for Measurement and Evaluation in Counseling and Development. (1989). *The responsibilities of users of standardized tests* (rev.). Washington, DC: Author.

American Counseling Association. (1988). *Ethical standards.* Alexandria, VA: Author.

American Psychological Association. (1985). *Standards for educational and psychological testing* (rev.). Washington, DC: Author.

American Rehabilitation Counseling Association, Commission on Rehabilitation Counselor Certification, and National Rehabilitation Counseling Association. (1995). *Code of professional ethics for rehabilitation counselors.* Chicago, IL: Author.

American School Counselor Association. (1992). *Ethical standards for school counselors.* Alexandria, VA: Author.

Joint Committee on Testing Practices. (1988). *Code of fair testing practices in education.* Washington, DC: Author.

National Board for Certified Counselors. (1989). *National Board for Certified Counselors code of ethics.* Alexandria, VA: Author.

Prediger, D. J. (Ed.). (1993, March). *Multicultural assessment standards.* Alexandria, VA: Association for Assessment in Counseling.

ACA INSURANCE TRUST

About the ACA Insurance Trust

The primary mission of the ACA Insurance Trust is to make a variety of quality insurance products available to ACA members. The ACA Insurance Trust strives to select and promote insurance programs that offer competitive rates and provide responsive customer service including efficient and equitable claim processing and underwriting.

A secondary mission of the Trust is to support ACA in ways that are consistent with the primary mission of the Trust.

ACA Insurance Trust, Inc., is made up of 10 trustees, 4 of whom are appointed by the ACA president on a rotating basis. The ACA president is also a voting trustee, and two outside trustees are appointed by an independent service company to add other expertise to the body. The ACA president-elect, ACA's executive director, and the trust's executive director serve as ex-officio members. The Trust employs a staff that is responsible for the administration and implementation of operations approved by the trustees.

Benefits of the ACA Professional Liability Insurance Program

- *Choice of Liability Limits.* The range goes from $200,000 per occurrence/$200,000 aggregate to $2,000,000 per occurrence/$4,000,000 aggregate.
- *Occurrence Protection.* Coverage for claims reported at any future time as long as the "incident" happened during an insured time period.
- *State Licensing Board Defense.* Up to $2,500 per policy period for expenses from the investiga-

tion or defense of a proceeding before state licensing or other review boards. Insured counselor may retain an attorney of their own choosing.

- *Premises Liability Coverage.* Provides protection for claims such as slips and falls in the operation of the offices used in the Insured's practice as a counselor.
- *Individual or Group Coverage.* Whether you are a formal corporation or loose-knit affiliation, added liability coverage can be obtained by having group protection. Discounts are available based on the size of the group.
- *Toll-free Risk Management Hotline.* Insured counselors may speak to an attorney when faced with situations that could lead to allegations of malpractice.
- *Discounts for Attending ACA Workshops on Ethics or Legal Aspects of Counseling.* 10% credit applied to new and renewal applications up to 2 years.
- *New Professional Discount.* Graduating Masters or Ph.D. students may deduct 25% from their premium the first year they work as professional counselors.
- *Quality Service from ACA Insurance Trust Staff.* They are highly trained insurance professionals who maintain constant dialogue with the Trust members and ACA so that insured members are given the best advantage in policy provisions, rates, and service.

Benefits of ACA-Sponsored Life and Health Plans

- *Economical Group Rates.* Administrative procedures are streamlined and the savings are passed on to ACA members.
- *Quality Service from the Administrator selected by the Trust.* The policy features were designed with the assistance of counseling professionals. The Trust members and staff stay on top of insurance industry developments and back up the members so they obtain the best possible policy and service.

Telephone inquiries are welcomed at 1-800-347-6647, Extension 284.

CHECKLIST: INFORMED WRITTEN CONSENT FOR TREATMENT

Requirements vary greatly regarding the necessity and/or the content of an informed written consent for treatment—sometimes referred to as a Fact Sheet. Agency or institutional policies, state counselor licensing laws and rules, and other binding directives often determine the existence and/or content of this document. The intent of an informed consent document is to define the basic treatment relationship between counselor and client. Misunderstanding and disappointment, which are often the genesis of a liability claim, can be reduced when clients are made knowledgeable of the ground rules of the counseling relationship. Trust and the therapeutic relationship are enhanced when clients understand what is expected and/or required of a counselor and of themselves in a successful counseling relationship.

The following topics are recommended for consideration when developing an informed written consent for treatment:

1. *Voluntary Participation.* Clients voluntarily agree to treatment and can terminate at any time without penalty.

2. *Client Involvement.* What level of involvement and what type of involvement will be expected from clients?

3. *Counselor Involvement.* What will the counselor provide? How will this be provided? How can the counselor be

---

From Bertram, B. & Wheeler, A. M. (1994). "Legal aspects of counseling: Avoiding lawsuits and legal problems" (Workshop material). Alexandria, VA: American Counseling Association.

THE COUNSELOR AND THE LAW

reached in the event of an emergency.

4. *No Guarantees.* Counselors cannot guarantee results (i.e., become happier, less tense or depressed, save the marriage, stop drug use, obtain a good job, etc.).

5. *Risks Associated with Counseling.* Define what, if any, risks are associated with the counselor's particular approach to counseling.

6. *Confidentiality and Privilege.* Specify how confidentiality will be handled in couple counseling, family counseling, child/adolescent counseling, and group counseling situations. How may confidential and privileged information be released.

7. *Exceptions of Confidentiality and Privilege.* Define specific statutory circumstances where confidentiality and privilege cannot be maintained (i.e., abuse reporting).

8. *Counseling Approach or Theory.* What is the counselor's counseling orientation or theoretical belief system? How will that affect treatment?

9. *Counseling and Financial Records.* What will the include? How long will they be maintained? How will they be destroyed?

10. *Ethical Guidelines.* What standard defines the counselor's

practice? How might a client obtain a copy of these guidelines?

11. *Licensing Regulations.* What license does the counselor hold? How may a client check on the status of the licensee?

12. *Credentials.* What education, training, and experience credential will the counselor need to provide counseling treatment, including any specialty credentials.

13. *Fees and Charges.* What are the specific fees and charges? How will fees be collected? How are financial records maintained?

14. *Insurance Reimbursement.* What responsibility will the counselor take for filing insurance forms? What fees, if any, are associated with insurance filing? How will co-payments be handled?

15. *Responsibility for Payment.* Who is responsible for payment of counseling charges? How will delinquent accounts be handled, what charges will be assessed for delinquent accounts?

16. *Disputes and Complaints.* How will fee or other disputes be resolved? Provide the address and phone number of the state licensing board for complaints if required by state licensing statute.

17. *Cancellation Policy.* How much notice for cancellation of a scheduled appointment is required? What fees will be charged for late cancellation?

18. *Affiliation Relationship.* Describe independent contractor and/or partnership relationship with any other practitioners in office suite.

19. *Supervisory Relationship.* Describe any required supervisory relationship along with reason for the supervision. Provide supervisor's name and credentials.

20. *Colleague Consultation.* Indicate that, in keeping with generally accepted standards of practice, you frequently consult with other mental health professionals regarding the management of cases. The purpose of the consultation is to ensure quality care. Every effort is made to protect the identity of clients.